How to use
Web 2.0
in your library

Phil Bradley

facet publishing

Published by Facet Publishing,
7 Ridgmount Street, London WC1E 7AE
www.facetpublishing.co.uk

Facet Publishing is wholly owned by CILIP: the Chartered Institute of
Library and Information Professionals.

British Library Cataloguing in Publication Data
A catalogue record for this book is available from the British Library.

ISBN 978-1-85604-607-7

First published 2007

Typeset from author's files in 11/15 pt University Old Style and
Zurich by Facet Publishing.
Printed and made in Great Britain by Cromwell Press Ltd,
Trowbridge, Wiltshire.

How to use
Web 2.0
in your library

Contents

Preface

Over the years I have been involved in writing, updating or editing some 14 books about various aspects of the internet, and I can honestly say that in many ways this title has been the most difficult but enjoyable to write. Not because the subject matter in and of itself is difficult – far from it: it's a reasonably straightforward matter to look at different resources and see how they may be used by information professionals – but because it's an area that is changing remarkably quickly. Enjoyable, because it is fast moving, and providing lots of opportunities for enthusiastic information professionals.

We are of course used to the speed of change on the internet – interfaces change almost as quickly as the wind direction, the resources that everyone appears to be talking about today are forgotten tomorrow, and improvements and new versions are taken for granted. With this book, however, the change was even more noticeable – the interfaces for several of the products that I refer to in the book have changed not just once but several times. Every single day, except perhaps for a couple of Sundays, I have discovered, been notified about or have found resources that I would like to have included in the book. Indeed, it's not just new resources – it is entirely new ideas and concepts that deserve consideration and discussion. As I am writing this preface the new gaming console the Wii has come onto the market, and one or two libraries have just started to make use of it; there are already a number of interesting discussions and examples of this.

However, it is an unfortunate but necessary fact of life that in order to get this book published I have to stop writing at some point. Consequently by the time you read this you may, quite understandably, ask yourself 'Why wasn't this resource included?' or 'Why didn't he cover that aspect?', and the answer in almost every case is down to time. Either that there wasn't enough of it, or that the particular resource wasn't actually available when the cut-off point for the book was reached, which for those of you with an interest in such things was 31 December 2006.

In order to reduce the impact that this rapid change will have on the contents of the book I have created a website (**www.zimbio.com/portal/ How+to+use+Web+2.0+in+your+library**), using some of the resources mentioned to allow you, the reader, not only to keep updated on changes, but to notify others of any changes that you find for yourself. This title is really just a starting point, and my hope is that it can be your entry point into an interesting, enjoyable community of other people who have also read the book, visited the website and added to the knowledge that is found there. So I would invite you to become involved yourself: please do visit this book's website (details in the Appendix) and keep up to date, or add your own comments, ideas, alterations and amendments. If there's a resource that you think is wonderful, add it. If you discover a new way of using an application within a library environment, point everyone towards it. If you discover that a URL in the book has changed, amend it in the appropriate section on the website.

The resources I have chosen to include in this title are based on a number of different criteria. If I use a product myself, have found that it materially changes the way in which I do something on the internet, and think it would be useful for other librarians and information professionals to use, I have in all probability included it. If other librarians talk about specific resources and have incorporated their use into their own weblogs, websites or ways of working I've also included them. If a colleague has seen a product and has been able to use it to enhance the service they provide, or that makes their job as an information professional slightly easier, I'm also likely to have included that as well. If I've seen an allusion to a product on a website or weblog that I trust, or that has won some sort of award, it may well get a mention.

Non-inclusion, however, does not mean that I or the general information community don't like a product: it may simply mean that not enough people have made enough of a fuss about it, or that it was too new to be included or at the time it was released it didn't appear to have any particular value for a library/information community. Once again I invite you to add anything to the website if you think that it will be of value or interest to colleagues. In fact, it is because I hope that you will get actively involved that I am slightly less concerned about omissions than I would have been otherwise, because I know that they can be rectified quickly and easily. This is one of the delights of working with Web 2.0, and with a community of enthusiastic information professionals. Having said all that, I am of course responsible for the choices that I have made regarding inclusion or otherwise in this title; if something has gone wrong then it's down to me, and I apologise in advance.

There are many people that I would like to thank for their help in the production of this title. All of the many hundreds of bloggers who keep me up to date and informed about new products and how they are using them. All of the people who have helped with the content of the book, by giving freely of their time and answering my questions. All of the people who are actually out there creating the products that we use on a regular or not so regular basis. Thanks also go to the organizations, both big and small, that I've taken screen-shots from; the copyright remains with them for all of them. I should add that every effort has been made to contact the copyright holders for permission; if there are any queries, please contact the publisher.

Particular thanks go to Sarah Houghton-Jan (the Librarian in Black), Michael Stephens, Gary Price, Danny Sullivan and all the British Librarian Bloggers – you may not have been aware of it, but your work is always inspirational, informative and valuable. Lastly, of course, most thanks go to my wife, Jill Bradley, for her understanding, love and support, to say nothing of the cups of tea she would bring, unbidden but just when needed. This book is, as always, dedicated to her.

Phil Bradley

Chapter 1

What is Web 2.0?

Introduction

As with most internet-related issues, if you try to find out what something means you often end up in a more confused state than when you started. The term Web 2.0 is clearly puzzling to a lot of people, and it was the most cited Wikipedia term of 2006, according to an article in *Advertising Age* at **http://adage.com/digital/article.php?article_id=114014**. The entry on Web 2.0 at **http://en.wikipedia.org/wiki/Web_2.0** states that the term 'refers to a perceived or proposed second generation of Internet-based services such as social networking sites, wikis, communication tools, and folksonomies that emphasize online collaboration and sharing among users'. Well, thanks for that – let's look elsewhere as well, shall we? I ran a search for the phrase 'Web 2.0 is' to see what would be retrieved. Among the various results were the following:

- harnessing collective intelligence
- a State of Mind
- a Buzzword!
- here today
- a threat to the venture capital model
- totally disruptive

- a marketing slogan
- bunk
- about finding new ways to interact on the internet and collaboration
- all about autonomous, distributed services, remixability
- a loose label for a variety of tools.

Clearly, therefore, whatever Web 2.0 is, it's not easy to pin down. In fact some would argue that it's a case of 'old wine in new bottles', and really doesn't exist as such, so it's necessary to search a little bit deeper to see if we can get any resolution on this. An article that is often referred to in the literature is 'What is Web 2.0', written by Tim O'Reilly and available at **www.oreillynet.com/pub/a/oreilly/tim/news/2005/09/30/what-is-web-20.html**, which goes into more detail. A number of core principles are discussed in the article, and it is worth while reading the whole piece to get a clearer indication of what many regard as *the* definition of Web 2.0

In many respects my own concern is much less to do with what Web 2.0 actually is or is not, and is rather based on the practical level of how various tools and applications can be used within a library or information centre. It just so happens that a lot of the tools that I'm looking at self-identify as Web 2.0 applications, so it is perhaps sensible to look at some of the criteria that these applications exhibit in order to obtain a clearer understanding of what exactly we're looking at.

Web 2.0 criteria

This should not be taken as a definitive listing of criteria, as I am sure that there are many exceptions and 'yes, buts' that could be introduced, but before we can proceed into the body of the book it will be helpful if you have some idea of what I regard as being a Web 2.0 based application.

The web as a platform

The majority of the resources that are mentioned in this book reside on the web itself. That is to say, you don't need to download them and install them on your own computer. In fact, if you did so their flexibility and value would be impaired to the extent that they would become almost worthless. Consider for a moment the situation in which you have to send around a document for colleagues to look at and perhaps edit. At the moment you could e-mail copies, whereupon everyone could make their own changes independently of one another (some of which I'm sure would be contradictory) and send them back to you to try to sort out the mess. Alternatively you could try to get everyone into a room together and thrash out the differences, which may simply be impracticable. Or you could make executive decisions yourself, then ask for comments again and the whole cycle would continue until someone called a halt – either that or the document would be out of date before publication!

In a Web 2.0 environment it is possible to put a document up onto the web and, using a web-based word processor, all your colleagues can make changes to it (which can be seen and rolled back if necessary) there and then. So, not only is the actual document itself shared, but the application (the word processor) is shared on the web as well.

Many of the resources that we'll be looking at in this book are used directly on the web. Alternatively, they will work with an application on your own system, so you could, for example, create a PowerPoint presentation, then upload it to a utility such as SlideShare at **www.slideshare.net** and allow comments or even edits online.

The advantage of this approach is that having your own desktop computer begins to become redundant: you do not need to use a specific workstation, because your files and projects are held elsewhere. Furthermore, with some products, such as start pages (which we'll be looking at in Chapter 5), you can use any computer, log onto 'your' start page and carry on working, irrespective of the place you happen to be. Mobility becomes a key issue at this point both in terms of you yourself, in that you can work just as well in the office, at home or on the train (given a suitable connection to the internet), and in terms of the data that you're using – by having it held centrally it is immediately accessible. The danger of course is that if that third-party resource goes down for whatever reason, you cannot get access to your data and will need to revert to back-up copies stored on a machine that is local to you. While I don't wish to deny that this is a drawback, equally I don't feel that it should stop people using such resources since, after all, computers themselves die, so back-ups are always a sensible precaution. I'd also make the point that while the third-party

resource may be inaccessible for a period of time, it is less likely that it will
be more reliable than a local computer, and back-ups of data will be made
more often.

Collective intelligence

Web 2.0 resources are often referred to as ways in which the 'wisdom of
the crowd' can be harnessed. I don't think that this should be taken entirely
literally, as after all if it were we'd all still think that the world was flat. On
the other hand, two heads are usually better than one. Many resources
mentioned in the forthcoming chapters work simply because lots of
people have had input into them. They have added 'tags' to help define
images or web pages, for example, making them easier to find, or they will
have edited and amended the content of an encyclopedia, or added
additional information to a community-based resource. Even on a fairly
basic level, the comments that people leave on various weblog entries can
illuminate, point readers in different directions, and provide additional
discussion points that the original author had not thought of.

Of course, there are dangers with this approach, and the regular
vandalism of articles in the Wikipedia mentioned in detail at
http://en.wikipedia.org/wiki/Wikipedia:Vandalism demonstrates this.
There is the question of trust inherent in letting a group of individuals
(many of whom you may not know) become involved with projects that
you are working on. This concept is often referred to as 'radical trust' and
is at least in part based on the concept that people will either do nothing
bad, or will act for the good of all. This isn't a new concept at all, of course
– we don't surround statues with barbed wire, and only in extreme cases
do people vandalize paintings.

The community therefore ceases to be a community that acts passively,
but becomes involved as a co-creator. In previous years all that people could
do would be to look at a web page, and maybe print it out, but they could
not affect it. If they disagreed with something they could create their own
web page, or mention it in a newsgroup or mailing list, but that was about
it. With many of the resources we'll be looking at in this book, the person
who disagrees with something can change it. The hope of course is that
they will be sensible in their amendments, but if they go overboard it is

almost always possible to replace their amended version with a previous version of a page or article. While radical trust is therefore a positive way to approach the creation of, or improvement to, a body of data, it does need to be tempered with functionality to ensure it cannot be abused.

It is also worth making the point that the user has a much richer experience when involved with Web 2.0 based resources. The role of the user is much more interesting and challenging now: users are able to combine materials for themselves to the extent that they do not need to know how to write websites, or gather data from different sources – the resources themselves take care of much of the technical side, while a user needs to think about what they want to create, which elements to fit into that whole process, and how they can provide an additional voice to other resources. Within a library context the involvement of the end-users is going to become a vital and integral part of providing new services. Now, we can always argue that the involvement of the user isn't new – no users means no library service! However, the point here is that users are becoming co-creators of content and adding to the overall experience. If a library produces a photographic record of an event, for example, users can add their own photographs, or perhaps an audio recording of something that happened at the event. While both the library and the user could do this independently if the two could work together, by creating a Flickr group, for example, the richness of the experience from both sides is enhanced. Librarians need to build this into the development of resources, and rather than limiting involvement they need to encourage and foster that enthusiasm by reaching out to the users.

The end of the software cycle

We're all now fairly used to seeing products in 'beta test mode' (that is to say in an unfinished test version) – Google, for example, often keeps products in that state for months if not years. Previously a company would work on a piece of software for a period of time, check it to make sure it was as bug-free as possible, and then release it or sell it as a 'finished' product. Of course, it wasn't finished since users would find bugs, or would suggest enhancements to the product and the developers would start the process again, releasing another 'finished' product 18 months later, whereupon the whole cycle would begin again. Web 2.0 based products tend to work on a rather different cycle, in that a product will be released to a waiting audience (or more realistically will just be released with the hope that the audience will simply turn up) and changes will be made as and when necessary.

Improvements or changes will therefore be ongoing, with the product growing organically and changing according to the needs of the users over the course of time. Users need to appreciate this is going to happen, and that very few things are going to be set in stone. It is quite common to use a product and then find it changed the next day, without any fanfare. This can be quite disconcerting if you are expecting that a product will stay the same over a long period of time. Of course, since it's unlikely that a user will be actually purchasing a product they can't control this, and need to get used to the idea that beta is in effect forever. We are now reaching a point where everything is changing all of the time, and traditional approaches no longer have a great deal of meaning. If someone writes a story in a weblog, for example, that story will immediately become available to millions of people, and the ability to sit and think about a response, to craft a carefully worded rebuttal, perhaps is not the way in which the situation can be dealt with any longer.

We need to move into a situation where 'good enough' becomes more important (and more effective) than 'perfect'. While the idea of perfection is something that is worth striving for it can become an obstacle. As information professionals we need to consider what resources will work for our clients today, to utilize them, promote them and then, if necessary, discard them tomorrow and move onto something else. This is very hard, because for many people change is a threat and is perceived as a bad thing, but in the new paradigm change is simply a way of life.

Having said that, I wouldn't want to give the impression that the resources mentioned here are constantly in a state of flux and are different every time you look at them. The ones mentioned in detail have generally been available for several months, if not years, and while they are not perfect, the development cycle has slowed down quite considerably. There is also a difference between a start-up product created by a small group of people (or even a single individual), and one that has matured over time, eventually being bought by one of the large corporations that can fold it into its body of offerings.

Technical issues

The technicalities of the development of these products is perhaps of less interest to librarians and other information professionals, and of more interest to developers of systems and resources, but it's worth making one or two points about them. One of the reasons that Web 2.0 products have developed so quickly is because of the advent of Ajax, otherwise known as Asynchronous JavaScript and XML. This is a development tool that combines a variety of other resources such as HTML (Hyper Text Markup Language), Cascading Style Sheets, JavaScript and so on. Once these are brought together it becomes possible to update various parts or elements of a web page instead of having to update the entire thing, or reloading the complete browser page.

What that means for the end-user is that a web page is no long a static page, or the electronic version of a printed page. It means that a page can be broken down into individual modules and these can be dragged, resized, changed and manipulated as necessary by the end-user. The user is therefore in control of their environment, which allows the creation of resources that are unique to that individual. It also means that resources can be combined in new and exciting ways into what are commonly referred to as 'mashups', and these are discussed in more detail in Chapter 11.

This functionality is further enhanced by the publication of APIs, or application programming interfaces. Some major companies such as Google, Yahoo! and Amazon allow people to use their API to take, manipulate and display data in different formats. The ability to quickly and easily create new products based on existing data is made much easier, and a good listing of examples can be found on the ProgrammableWeb site at **www.programmableweb.com**.

The Web 2.0 challenge for libraries

This is a subject that I'll look at in more detail in Chapter 12, in particular when I look at Library 2.0, but it is worth bringing up in this first chapter since the question of 'All this Web 2.0 stuff is all very well, but is it relevant to me?' is a justifiable and important one. You'll notice here that I'm talking about Web 2.0 as a challenge *for* libraries, and not a challenge *to* libraries.

What many of these resources will allow, and indeed encourage, is outreach. The librarian has been moving away from the 'gatekeeper to knowledge' for a very long time now. One of the reasons that CD-ROM-based databases proved so popular is because they allowed users to access material for themselves, run their own searches and keep up to date from their own desks, without needing to constantly come down to the library, or ask the librarian to intervene in the data-collection process on their behalf. Of course, this did not mean that the librarian became less important – in fact, on the contrary, the role has become even more important, because it is the librarian who is responsible for teaching end-users how to work effectively in the gathering of data, to choose the most appropriate resources, and to deploy them within the organization.

The internet has encouraged that decentralization, while at the same time providing information professionals with the ability to follow through with that movement, and reach out to users in ways that have not been possible before. As we shall see throughout the rest of the book, almost every single Web 2.0 resource can be used to make the life of the information professional less complicated in their day-to-day work and in their own professional updating, but also allows librarians to quickly and easily create new resources for their users. Importantly they are able to do this themselves, without having to wait for technical support to get involved: the strength of the professional is in their understanding of the knowledge, value and distribution of data, and Web 2.0 simply encourages this. To that extent I would say that Web 2.0 – and Library 2.0 – is a new concept and something that is entirely different and quite radical, because it puts the technical control and development of resources right in the hands of the librarian in an unprecedented way. On the other hand, providing information, keeping in direct contact with clients, and running updating and selective dissemination of information services are something that librarians have been doing for centuries.

Conclusion

Librarians want to provide information and answers to clients. They have a curiosity about everything and a keenness to interact with people, and a desire to make the lives of others that much easier. Their role within an organization cannot be overlooked – it is tremendously important, and all of the resources discussed in this book assist in this whole process. Web 2.0, however you define it, is providing new and interesting resources for librarians to continue to do what they have always done so well in the past – bringing order out of chaos and making information readily available. Let's take a look at how we can do it.

URLs mentioned in this chapter

http://adage.com/digital/article.php?article_id=114014
http://en.wikipedia.org/wiki/Web_2.0
http://en.wikipedia.org/wiki/Wikipedia:Vandalism
www.oreillynet.com/pub/a/oreilly/tim/news/2005/09/30/what-is-web-
    20.html
www.programmableweb.com
www.slideshare.net

Chapter 2

RSS

Introduction

It's almost impossible to browse the internet these days without seeing mention of RSS, or icons pointing to RSS resources. RSS really is the glue that holds a lot of Web 2.0 resources together – in fact many of the utilities that are referred to in the book simply would not work without RSS.

One of the nice things about RSS is that you don't actually need to know a great deal about it. In the same way that you don't need to know how HTML works in order to view pages, you can utilize RSS functionality without knowing anything about it – in fact it's quite possible that you're already using it in one form or another without being aware of it.

RSS stands for Rich Site Summary, Really Simple Syndication, RDF (Resource Description Framework) Site Summary or even Read Some Stories, depending on whom you talk to. (There is also another form of RSS that is referred to as ATOM, the main difference being that ATOM is rather more complex. In most instances this is all you'll ever need to know about the difference, but if you're interested I would suggest visiting AtomEnabled at **www.atomenabled.org**). Sometimes you'll also see RSS files labelled as RDF, but once again for our purposes this is only of interest to people who like to get 'under the hood' with technical details; you only need to know this because you may see files (such as the one in Figure 2.1, in fact) referenced as .rdf, but they're essentially exactly the same thing.

At its simplest level RSS is a series of different tags, usually things such as a title, an author, a summary and a link to a web page. The clever thing about RSS is that although content can appear in a wide variety of different formats, such as a weblog or a news feed from the BBC, or discussions in a bulletin board system, the underlying feed created in RSS means that the data can quickly be moved from one resource to another and displayed in a variety of different ways. This makes much more sense if we use a visual example. Figure 2.1 is a screen-shot from my weblog, but it could easily have been almost anyone else's weblog, or a screen-shot from a BBC news page. At the risk of stating the obvious, you can read it – that's what it's designed for. However, there is a second version of this page, and I'll include only a tiny segment because it probably won't make any sense at all, as you'll see from Figure 2.2. You may be able to make out a few words here or there, and if you're familiar with HTML it will make more sense. The important point, however, is that I am now in a position to take this data and use it with a number of other utilities and resources that work with the RSS format.

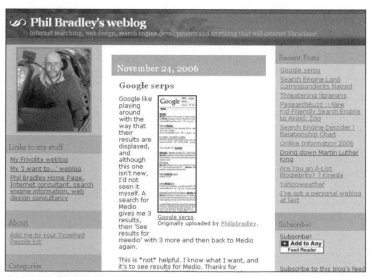

Figure 2.1 The author's weblog

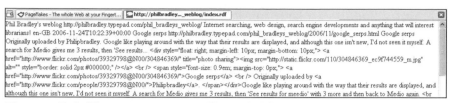

Figure 2.2 The same content as Figure 2.1 from the same source but in an RSS format

I can include the content of my weblog on my home page, for example. There are a number of utilities that allow subscribers (paying or otherwise) to point to an RSS feed and then incorporate it into a straightforward HTML web page. The one that is in use here is provided by Feed Digest at **www.feeddigest.com** and it works very simply – just provide it with the address of a particular feed and it will provide a piece of HTML to cut and paste onto a web page.

Figure 2.3 shows this in action: although the physical appearance of the content is completely different – it is now just a simple list of headings from recent weblog posts, the image has been lost, and the formatting is completely different – the actual information is exactly the same. A user can click on a heading that catches their eye and they will then be directed to the original posting at the weblog itself. Another good example of how this can be used is with the news feeds from the BBC: they can be incorporated directly into a web page, so a website author can provide his or her readers with up-to-the-minute news about a particular subject.

An even more common and perhaps even more useful way to utilize RSS feeds is to include them in a news reader or news aggregator. This is

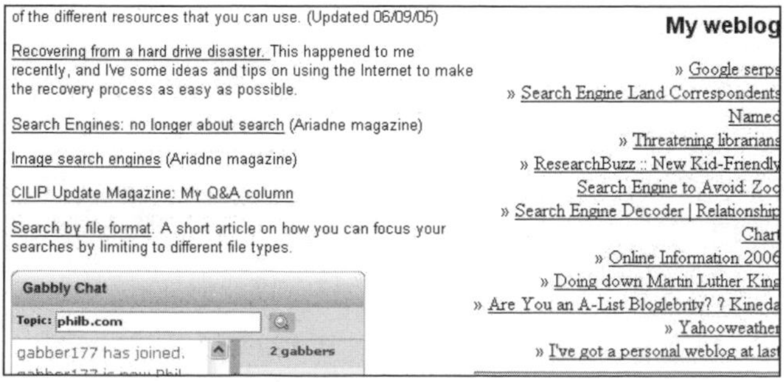

Figure 2.3 The author's weblog displayed on his home page

a resource that takes a large number of feeds and displays them, again
usually in a simplified form, for the user to quickly glance through, stop
at any headline that is of interest, and then click and view the original
content in a new browser window. There are a great many different types
of RSS reader but they all work in essentially exactly the same way. So,
at the risk of repetition, my weblog displays as you can see in Figure 2.4
using the Bloglines reader (**www.bloglines.com**).

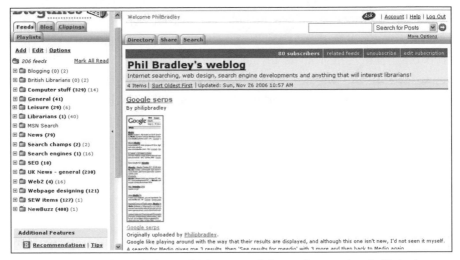

Figure 2.4 The same post as shown in Figure 2.1 displayed in Bloglines

If you thought that was flexible, there are still other ways in which an RSS
feed can be displayed. Browsers can also be used to display data as live
feeds, and all that a user needs to do is use the 'Bookmark' or 'Favorites'
list to see the headlines that are available. Figure 2.5 shows how this can
look within the Firefox browser, and the latest version of Microsoft
Internet Explorer (version 7) displays RSS feeds in a similar fashion.

There are plenty of other ways in which RSS feeds can be used, but
hopefully the previous examples have illustrated just a few of the things
that can be done with them. However, if you're keen to learn more about
them and other ways you use them, you'll find the chapter on start pages
(Chapter 5) particularly interesting. They really are an extraordinary way

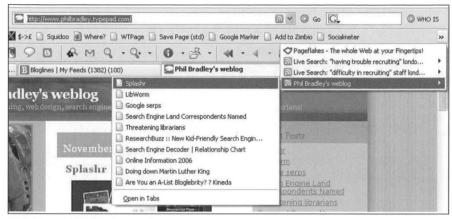

Figure 2.5 An RSS feed displayed in Firefox

of sharing data simply and easily, and indeed many people are claiming that 'RSS is the future'.

Identifying RSS feeds

Before you can start using RSS feeds you need to be able to recognize them, of course. Luckily this is a reasonably simple task, although as usual with anything to do with the internet there is never one single straightforward way of doing something! There are a number of icons that are worth looking out for on different pages that you visit.

Figure 2.6
Different icons indicating the availability of an RSS feed

Figure 2.6 shows a few examples of the icons you'll see on pages that indicate that there is an RSS version available. They'll often have white text with a bright orange background, but it's not entirely unusual to see a blue background instead. Another place to look for RSS icons is in the address bar of the browser, and Figure 2.7 shows the URL of the BBC news page in Firefox with the RSS icon clearly shown at the extreme right.

Figure 2.7 The BBC news page with the RSS icon at the right-hand side

Once you have identified a page that contains an RSS feed you have an interest in viewing, it becomes necessary to decide exactly how you want to view it. You may already have got a few ideas from this chapter already, but the next sections will explain how to properly utilize RSS in a number of different ways.

Using RSS feeds in an RSS feed reader

I'm sure you're expecting me to say that there are a great many RSS readers available to you, and the problem lies in not finding one, but in narrowing down all of the different options to a single choice. If you are thinking that – you're absolutely right! Luckily most RSS readers work in very similar ways, so the choice is down to personal preference, rather than having to choose one function over another. Since the vast majority of readers (or aggregators, depending on your choice of term) are free you can try out a number of them quickly and easily, discarding the ones that you don't feel comfortable with. If you're worried that you will have wasted a lot of time and energy in creating a collection of feeds, do not be concerned, because the majority of readers will allow you to export that collection in what is known as an OPML (Outline Processor Markup Language) file which can be stored on your hard disk and then imported into another reader without any problem.

Most advanced readers will do considerably more than just offer to display RSS feeds for you: you can use them to create your own weblogs, or have news clippings from particular posts and so on. Owing to space constraints I won't go into considerable detail on all these different functions; after all, you'll want something to explore for yourself, and so I will just look at some of the basic options.

Bloglines

Bloglines, which is to be found at **www.bloglines.com**, has been available since 2003; it was acquired by Ask.com in February 2005. It is free, although you do need to register in order to use it. The main Bloglines screen can be seen in Figure 2.4, although when you first register with Bloglines the list of folders on the left-hand side of the screen will be rather smaller – it's worth pointing out that the image is of my collection of feeds, so yours will of course be rather different. The process of getting feeds into the reader is very straightforward and, as you will probably be expecting by now, there are various methods available to you. Bloglines offers an easy 'subscribe' bookmarklet (similar to a bookmark, but instead of taking you to a specific web page it executes a particular function) that you install in your browser, and once you find a feed that you're interested in, simply click on the bookmarklet and it will prompt you, as shown in Figure 2.8. Simply click on the appropriate boxes according to your own preferences (you'll probably want to play around with the options to begin with to see what they all do), and then sit back with Bloglines doing the work of updating your feed from then on – generally once an hour.

Figure 2.8 Subscribing to the UK BBC News RSS feed with Bloglines

Many site authors will make life even easier by offering an 'easy subscribe' button on their weblog or news feed: Figure 2.9 (overleaf) shows the weblog Search Engine Land, at **http://feeds.searchengineland.com/ searchengineland**, which offers multiple ways of subscribing to the news feed, depending on the particular news reader being employed. You'll see that there is an option to subscribe via Bloglines in the collection of icons and it

Search Engine Land: News About Search Engines & Search Marketing
syndicated content powered by FeedBurner

FeedBurner makes it easy to receive content updates in My Yahoo!, Newsgator, Bloglines, and other news readers.

Learn more about syndication and FeedBurner...

Subscribe Now!

...with web-based news readers. Click your choice below:

[MY YAHOO!] [newsgator] [MY AOL]
[Rojo] [BLOGLINES] [netvibes]
[Add to Google] [PAGEFLAKES]

...with other readers:

[(Choose Your Reader) ▼]

Get Search Engine Land: News About Search Engines & Search Marketing delivered by email

View Feed XML

Screen-shot reproduced with thanks.

Figure 2.9 Various options provided by Search Engine Land to add its feed to different readers, such as Bloglines (second row, middle icon)

is a simple matter to click on it: this opens Bloglines and you can once again add the news feed directly.

If all else fails, you can ask Bloglines to hunt around and see if it can find a feed for you. Simply click on the 'Add' option in the menu bar on the left-hand side of the screen (which you can see in Figure 2.10) and type in the address of the weblog or news source you wish to add. Bloglines will then do its best to identify a feed for you.

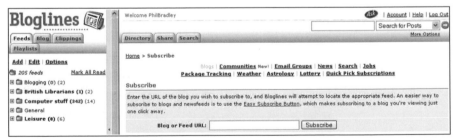

Figure 2.10 Adding a news feed manually with Bloglines

Alternatively, you may sometimes be given the option of viewing the RSS feed directly: Figure 2.9 shows that option at Search Engine Land with the RSS icon and 'View Feed XML'. Click on that link, and then cut and paste the resulting URL into the Bloglines subscribe box and let the software take care of the rest.

Once you have collected a number of feeds you will probably want to allocate them to different folders to group similar subject areas together. Just click on the 'Edit' option, seen at the top of the left-hand column, in Figure 2.10, and create folders appropriate to your interests: you can then simply click and drag feeds into the folders. It's simple to add more folders, change their names and move feeds from one to another, so feel free to explore and experiment.

Using your RSS reader is as simple as visiting a website: just sign in, click on a folder and the software will then display new posts in the main right-hand pane. You can keep any items that interest you for later consideration by clicking on the 'Keep New' box, and that item will display every time you view the folder. The default action of a reader is to delete posts once they have been displayed since the whole point of the operation is to give you new material, rather than cluttering up older posts with new data. However, previous posts can be retrieved by telling Bloglines to display all postings within a specific period of time.

Bloglines will update itself generally every hour, which for most of us should be enough, but you may find other readers will update at different time periods. I generally leave my Bloglines page open as a tab or background window all the time so that I can dip in and out whenever I have a minute to spare, but you may prefer to get into a habit of just checking once or twice a day. Remember that the emphasis is on the 'here and now' - if you want older material you should be using a traditional search engine! The number of feeds you take should be limited by the amount of time you have available; I generally take somewhere in the region of 200 feeds, but Bloglines has reported the largest number of feed subscriptions that any one person takes is over 1400. It's easy to subscribe to feeds and just as easy to unsubscribe, and you should be determined about this - if you find that a feed isn't as helpful or as informative as you hoped, then simply unsubscribe. If you notice that you're not looking at a particular folder, or it's getting a lot of unread posts in it, then simply delete the lot; if you don't read them there's no point having them. In other words - develop a ruthless streak when it comes to subscribing and unsubscribing from feeds or weblogs.

The Google RSS Reader

If you use Google for a variety of other internet-related activities (searching, e-mail, etc.) you may wish to use it as your news reader as well. The Google RSS Reader can be found at **www.google.com/reader** and it works in a very similar fashion to Bloglines, or indeed any other reader that's available. Figure 2.11 illustrates the similar look and feel of the services.

Users can create a list of feeds that they take, and can quickly recommend various posts or sites to their friends. They can keep useful items on their own personalized page, which creates a whole series of links and information on matters of interest to you, and of course friends and colleagues can subscribe to this list as well. All that is necessary is to click on the sharing icon, and Google automatically provides you with a URL and the entire article is then made available for reading. The Google Reader can be used on a mobile phone (depending on the functionality of the phone), so you can always stay right up to date with new and breaking stories.

The Google Reader also displays data in chronological format, so it's very compact and easy to scroll through, as you can see in Figure 2.12. If something takes your interest it's easy to flick back and forth between list and expanded viewpoint.

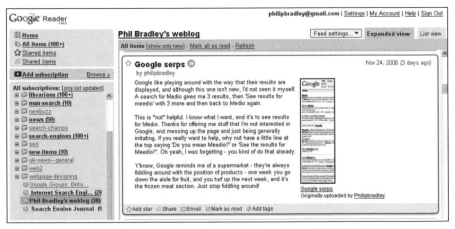

Screen-shot reproduced with thanks.

Figure 2.11 The Google Reader interface

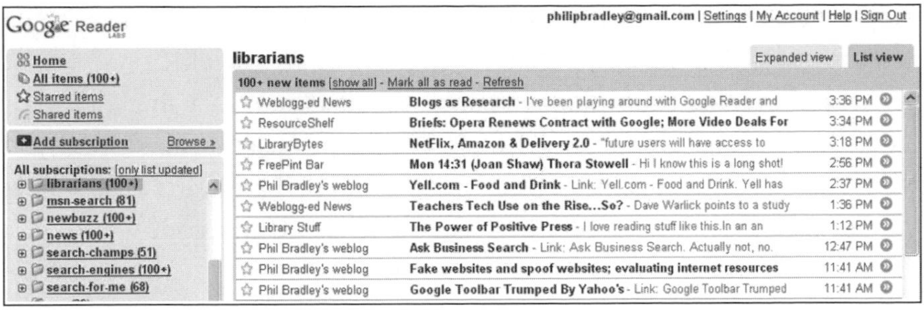

Screen-shot reproduced with thanks.

Figure 2.12 The Google Reader in List (chronological) view

Other RSS readers

When looking at RSS readers I could almost believe that there is a different reader available for anyone who wants one – there really are hundreds of them. They all exhibit slightly different characteristics, and while I've demonstrated briefly two of the most well known readers there are plenty more options available to you if you want to explore further.

There is a splendid collection of readers at the RSS Compendium at **http://allrss.com/rssreaders.html** which is organized according to operating system. The Google Directory offers several dozen readers at **http://directory.google.com/Top/Reference/Libraries/Library_and_Infor mation_Science/Technical_Services/Cataloguing/Metadata/RDF/ Applications/RSS/News_Readers**, and a collection is available at Yahoo! if you visit **http://dir.yahoo.com/Computers_and_Internet/Data_ Formats/XML__eXtensible_Markup_Language_/RSS/RSS_Readers_and_ Aggregators**.

Even more RSS tools

At the risk of making you even more giddy, there are various other RSS tools that are available, doing some very interesting things. It is possible to create a single RSS feed out of a number of other feeds: suppose that you have a collection of feeds from British librarians, or you like reading weblogs about alternative health. You can, and probably will, have these set up in your RSS reader as individual feeds, and this works very well if you have a specific interest in the author of the feed, but sometimes you may just want to have the data delivered to you irrespective of source. There are two useful tools here that do exactly that – KickRSS at **www. kickrss.com** takes multiple feeds and displays them as a single page or feed at an easy-to-remember URL. This becomes useful therefore if you want to make data available to other people, but perhaps don't have a great deal of interest in it yourself. RSS Mix at **www.rssmix.com** works in a similar way, and this resource allows you to share it on your web page quickly and easily.

It is also possible to create RSS feeds from those web pages that do not already have such a resource. Feedity at **www.feedity.com** simply requires users to input a URL and the resource will then visit the page and create a feed based on the content that it finds there; users of the service can then further refine that to include only those elements of a page that they are specifically interested in. Ponyfish at **www.ponyfish.com** and FeedYes at **www.feedyes.com** work in the same way. Alternatively, if a web author has their own site and wants to create an RSS feed from the content that will be of benefit to their readers, that can also be simply achieved using a resource such as RSSpect, at **www.rsspect.com**. Invisible markup tags are added to their content around those elements that are to be included in a feed, and the software takes care of everything else.

These resources, and others like them, are often referred to as 'scraper services'. A scraper does exactly what the name implies, which is to say that it visits a particular site or page, takes content such as headlines or titles, and places them into an RSS form, even if this wasn't the intention of the original author. They are not perfect, but they can often provide access to information that would otherwise be rather more laborious to collect manually.

Using RSS

Hopefully by now you will have got some idea of RSS and exactly what it does and, to some extent, how it does it (although the 'how' is much less important for our concerns and interests than the 'what'). I would strongly advise spending some time with a few of the resources mentioned above, though, just to get it clear in your own mind before you progress with the rest of this chapter. RSS really is such a powerful and all-pervasive technology, with so many possibilities, that you do need to get to grips with it, and the best way of doing that of course is to try it out. However, if we assume that you've put this book down and explored a little and have come back, let's take a more in-depth look at how you can harness the power of RSS for yourself, before looking at how it can be used more widely by a library or information centre.

Keeping up to date

Probably the single most useful thing that you can do with RSS feeds is use them to keep up to date with those weblogs or news feeds that you want to read on a regular basis. Rather than continually having to go back to a particular website or section at the BBC website, simply set up an RSS feed and then sit back and relax; the news will come to you, without you needing to go and chase it for yourself. The number of feeds that you choose will obviously depend on the amount of time that you have available, but obviously if you find that you're spending too long reading them you need to cut down on a few, or any that remain unread for a long time could be safely cut.

Automating searches

Not all search engines allow automated searches as an option at the moment, but they are becoming more popular. There may well be searches that you wish to do on a regular basis to keep up to date with what's happening in a subject area of interest, and you may – until now – have been doing them manually. This can be annoying because unless a search engine has an option to rearrange data by date you may see exactly the same information over and over as the results ranking will be based on relevance, not currency. However, this is beginning to change. When you run a search just check to see if an RSS feed or icon is displayed. Live at **www.live.com** offers RSS feeds for searches that you run, for example. Simply cut and paste the RSS URL into your news aggregator and save it. The aggregator will then run the search for you on a regular basis and will retrieve new data, rather than material that you have previously seen. It's also possible to do the same thing with Google, although it's a little more complicated. Start by visiting Google News at **http://news.google.com** and run a search. Next, look for the RSS link, and if you click on that you will get an RSS feed page for the search. Again, cut and paste that into your news aggregator and the news search has been created as an RSS feed for you. IceRocket at **www.icerocket.com** allows users to run searches (in weblogs, web pages, news or images, for example) and to save a search as an RSS feed.

There are various other resources and search engines that can be used to create search feeds. If you have an interest in weblogs themselves, it is worth visiting Technorati at **www.technorati.com**, Sphere at **www.sphere.com** or Topix at **www.topix.net** and creating feeds as previously described. In fact, if you're searching almost any resource now, it's worth checking to see if there is an RSS feed option available to you. For example, Furl at **www.furl.net** and del.icio.us at **www.delicious.com** that we'll be looking at in the social bookmarking chapter both provide users with the option to run and then save searches in an RSS format.

Watching specific pages

RSS feeds can be created to do little more than keep you informed about when a page is updated, but this can of course be extremely useful in its own right. For example, one very useful resource, the FreePint Bar – a forum for librarians to post questions and comments – has an RSS feed at **http://web.freepint.com/forum/bar/list.php** that keeps subscribers informed about additional postings to the service. I can therefore subscribe to this and only actually visit the site when I see a question that I find to be of some interest. The previously mentioned RSSpect resource provides a function whereby a specific URL can be monitored for any changes, and the alert is passed on via RSS rather than an e-mail.

The auction site eBay is very popular, and people will often automate searches for items of interest using their internal alerting service, but it's also possible to create an RSS feed that does exactly the same thing using RSSAuction at **www.rssauction.com**. Real addicts can have searches run every single hour just on the off-chance that that elusive piece of pottery is put up for auction.

Download.com at www.download.com is a site that offers users the opportunity to download free software, and it also has an RSS feed available that keeps subscribers up to date on what's available. The same thing can be done at Flickr, the photograph-sharing website at **www.flickr.com**, which has feeds for various different options, such as groups, discussions and specific individuals' photograph streams. You can read more about Flickr in Chapter 10. If you need to know what the weather is going to be like for a specific area there are many ways to find that data, but there is a site dedicated to providing that information in an RSS format – RSSWeather at **www.rssweather.com**. You merely need to go to the site, choose the area that interests you and you'll be taken to a page that offers that data, together with an RSS feed for it.

E-mail

Another surprising thing that you can do with RSS that many people are not aware of is to use it to collect and view your e-mail. Bloglines lets you create e-mail addresses that show up as subscriptions in your system and once you have done that you can subscribe to various feeds or mailing lists with that address. Alternatively you could use a product such as MailBucket at **www.mailbucket.org**: if you forward your e-mail to the account you establish there the service will generate an RSS feed for you. If you're a bit of a technical wizard you might want to try Mailfeed at **http://wiki.wonko. com/software/mailfeed**, which is a PHP script that checks POP3, IMAP and NNTP boxes on request. (If that didn't make any sense at all, don't worry, but don't bother to look at the resource either!) Alternatively, if you prefer e-mail to RSS there are resources that take a feed and turn it into an e-mail for you. RMail at **www.r-mail.org** and era at **http://era.indecorous. com/e-mail.html** are both resources that you can use for this purpose.

Miscellaneous resources

A lot of website owners have realized that by providing RSS they are in fact leveraging their own site's value and importance. It's not possible to provide a full listing, but here are some examples to give a flavour of the possibilities. For example, you can check virus alerts from Sophos at **http://sophos.com**, or Virus Bulletin at **www.virusbtn.com/support/feeds/ index.xml**. Eventful at **http://eventful.com** provides RSS feeds for events that are happening in particular cities around the world, so you'll always be able to find something to do on a Friday night. Jobs are advertised on the Monster website at **http://monster.com/Monster.com** – just follow the link to your own country and subscribe to an RSS feed for positions that interest you. Rethink(IP) at **www.rethinkip.com** provides an RSS feed for American patent applications, which is obviously a quick and easy way to keep up to speed in your area of interest. If you're based in the UK, Just the Flight at **www.justtheflight.co.uk/rss/flights.html** provides cheap last-minute flight offers via RSS either by airport or destination. Finally, RSS has many leisure uses as well, and if you enjoy comics it's worth taking a look at Comic Alert! at **www.comicalert.com** and the Webcomic List at **www.thewebcomiclist.com**, both of which do a good job in alerting you to new editions of your favourites.

Using RSS in a library setting

As a consumer of data produced by RSS there is therefore much that can be done, and even if an information professional went no further than collecting data and information via RSS they would undoubtedly be doing a better and more effective job in this area than previously. However, for the keen and enthusiastic information professional the value of RSS goes far beyond that of a mere consumer – it is now possible for the professional to become the publisher, far more easily than before. Librarians have been publishers on the net for many years now, ever since the first library web page appeared, but publishing in this way is very often a slow and laborious process, often requiring the input of a technical member of staff to code web pages and take the librarian's content and render it into something that can be displayed on a screen. RSS is relatively easy to use, and if you recall my earlier outline of RSS it allows us to take data that is in one format and put it into another. Some of the functionality that we'll be looking at in the rest of this chapter will only really begin to make sense when you've also read about some of the other resources later in the book. You may well want to dip backwards and forwards in order to juggle your understanding of the subject matter, or you might simply wish to plough straight on, trusting that it will all come together shortly!

Incorporating content onto your site

As we have seen already in this chapter, it's possible to take third-party content, such as the various feeds from the BBC, and read them using a news aggregator. However, it's also possible, and indeed encouraged by a lot of publishers, to take that content and place it onto your own site. The BBC provides information on how to do this on its own site at **http://news.bbc.co.uk/shared/bsp/hi/services/htmlsyndication/html/ default.stm**, and it also explains that it's possible to create your own searches from its own search engine. Consequently you could take a BBC news feed that provides current information about your local region, and perhaps create a web page on your own library site entitled 'News about our area', for example. This has been done to great effect by the library service at the University of Winnipeg in Canada on its site at **http:// cybrary.uwinnipeg.ca**, while the Nashville Community High School provides both local and world news at **http://209.174.209.6/ nashville/library/news.htm**, for example. Alternatively, if you have a group of users who are particularly interested in a subject you could run a search on the BBC site, limit the results to news or sport, for example, and then use the RSS feed that you've created and embed it onto your own site.

We can, however, go much further than that: as we've already seen, some of the major search engines are providing users with the opportunity of creating a search and then viewing and keeping up to date with the results via RSS. Consequently you could have web pages on your site that pull in information from a wide variety of different search engines, all displaying current content, based on your expert ability to create tightly focused searches. Within a matter of minutes you could have your own press-cutting-service-cum-current-awareness-bulletin-cum-selective-dissemination-of-information resource all rolled into one. Your users can then just visit the appropriate web page and scan the news for useful items of interest. Examples of sites that do exactly this are the Daily Rotation at **www.dailyrotation.com**, which provides information from over 300 technical sites, and Detod at **http://my.detod.com** for legal information. At the other end of the spectrum, my own website at **www.philb.com** provides you with a feed that is limited to my own weblog. A nice example of a specialist organization doing much the same thing is the Institute of Physics, which has a collection of channels of RSS feeds for journals at **http://syndication.iop.org/?site**.

Now, is it really that easy, or are you expecting a very large 'but' at this point? It *is* almost that easy in actual fact – in order for all this to happen properly quite a lot of very complex work has to go on in the background, but luckily you don't need to know what exactly is going on. There are a great many resources that will allow you to either point to a specific source, such as a weblog or an RSS feed created by running a search on an appropriate search engine, and they will then create a feed for you, provide you with the HTML code – then it's simply a case of cutting and pasting that onto a web page. Feedzilla at **www.feedzilla.com** is a commercial product offering feeds and various other options in a variety of pricing models, and Newsfeed Maker at **www.newsfeedmaker.com** allows you to create feeds from a number of different resources based on your own keywords. Feed Digest at **www.feeddigest.com** will take feeds and put them onto your site, mix various feeds and create dashboards, for example. Alternatively you may want to try resources such as Grazr at **http://grazr.com**, Feedostyle at **www.feedostyle.com**, Feed2JS at **http://feed2js.org** or RSS to JavaScript at **www.rss-to-javascript.com**. If you wish to explore further, visit your favourite search engine and search on terms such as 'RSS syndication <your website>', which should provide you with results that include other tools.

Keeping people up to date with what you're doing

Another obvious way in which librarians can make use of RSS is in conjunction with their weblogs. Clearly this is a large topic that deserves more consideration than I'm able to give it here, so I'll return to this subject in Chapter 3. However, it's worth bearing in mind at this point that whatever it is that you do within your information centre, be it getting new resources, introducing a new member of staff, identifying and highlighting specific resources to help clients answer queries, all of this can be made available via RSS feeds.

It is also possible to create your own RSS feeds out of the traditional pages that you may have on your own website by using the scraper services mentioned earlier in this chapter. The idea of a web page being a fairly static piece of information, like a page in a book, is now really becoming outdated, since that information can be made to work for you much more than it ever has done in the past. While you may have put up information onto the page about what you or your information centre is doing, you did of course rely on your users coming to visit you to catch up – and even with the best will in the world people have a lot of calls on their time. However, by providing an RSS feed of the page that users can subscribe to, that visit now becomes less important, since you can push new information directly towards your users in a much more targeted fashion. I will not of course deny the fact that for this to work correctly users do need to buy into the concept of using RSS and news aggregators, so it could be argued that this is simply moving the problem elsewhere, but since using news feeds is such a time saver it shouldn't be too hard a job to persuade colleagues to at least consider using such a system.

Another resource that you may wish to explore is the use of a calendar to keep people current with what the library is doing. Rather than simply use a calendar on your own computer there are a number of Web 2.0 based calendars that can be created which will allow users to see when the library is open or closed, when particular events are taking place and so on. Not only is the calendar available online, but users can subscribe to the RSS feed that accompanies it, so they are always up to date with what is going on. Examples of some services that offer this option are Planzo at **http://demo.planzo.com**, 30 Boxes at **http://30boxes.com**, HipCal at **www.hipcal.com** or Mosuki at **http://mosuki.com**.

Providing feeds for other people

Another option available to an information centre is simply to make RSS feeds available directly to users for them to pick and choose which ones they wish to subscribe to. If you already have pages on your website that link to other sites and resources – and these days most libraries do – you should consider adding links to RSS-based feeds. This may involve slightly more work to explain to users that they're not going to be visiting a 'normal' web page if they click on a link, but that they'll be opening an RSS feed. This will require an explanation of exactly what RSS is, together with perhaps a link to a few readers, but the extent to which you get involved in that process is obviously up to you and your users. However, it is an option that is worth considering.

If you use any of the social bookmarking services, such as del.icio.us or Furl (which are discussed in more detail in Chapter 6), you can create RSS feeds for those. These could either be made available simply as a feed that a user could subscribe to, or they could be incorporated in a web page. If you're as yet unfamiliar with social bookmarking services you may simply want to hold this as a thought, or jump forward and read the chapter now and then return. However, if you're keen to keep reading here, social bookmarking services are, in a nutshell, the opportunity to share your bookmarks or favourites with other people. Consequently, if you have specific subject areas that you cover you may wish to consider bookmarking sites to make them available for researchers in that subject area. As it is a simple process to take a feed from a resource such as del.icio.us and it does not add to the amount of time that you take to add something to your own bookmark collection on your own computer, there is nothing to stop you from producing your own little index of top-quality websites that may be of use to other people.

Utilizing content from commercial providers

Commercial publishers of data clearly have a role to play in the greater provision of their material and content for their subscribers, or indeed to 'tempt' non-subscribers into considering their offerings. Consequently it is worth while looking at some of the commercial services that you use to see if they offer any kind of RSS service that you can utilize. Ingenta Connect provides feeds to alert users to the existence of new issues of journals, with tables of contents, abstracts and so on. This is explained in more detail on its website at **www.ingentaconnect.com/about/ researchers/subscribing_to_rss_feeds**. The Engineering Village at **www.engineeringvillage2.org**, which provides access to engineering content for engineers, students, researchers and information professionals, offers access to data via RSS feeds. Sage Journals Online also provides RSS feeds for current and recent issues, as it explains at **http://rss.sagepub. com/rss**. ProQuest further offers RSS-based resources – and you can read about them at **www.proquest.co.uk/syndication/rss**: 'ProQuest is one of the first aggregators to utilize RSS feeds. It is an easy way for customers to create valuable, in-context links to their ProQuest subscription content. This enables customers to enhance services to their users by integrating the latest articles in a particular field into the corresponding e-resources page on their library website.' The IEEE offers RSS feeds for its journals and periodicals which are available for anyone to subscribe to, with more details at **http://ieeexplore.ieee.org/xpl/periodicals.jsp**. Finally, although it's not a commercial publisher in the same way, it's possible to use databases such as PubMed at **www.ncbi.nlm.nih.gov/ entrez/query.fcgi?DB=pubmed** to run a search and then save the results into an RSS feed, as can be seen in Figure 2.13.

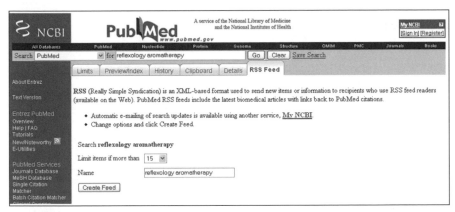

With thanks to the National Library of Medicine.

Figure 2.13 Saving a PubMed search to an RSS feed

Conclusion

As I hope I have been able to demonstrate, RSS is one of the absolute fundamentals of a Web 2.0 environment. Without RSS either many of the tools that we have mentioned, and will be discussing in the rest of this book, would not work at all, or their use and value would be so limited as to make them almost useless.

RSS has swiftly become one of the major elements of the internet, along with e-mail and web pages. Increasing numbers of information services utilize the value of it, and new resources incorporate it into the way that they work automatically. Although it's not the easiest thing to grasp, and the differing names have not helped its cause (and I suspect that before very long the word 'feed' or 'newsfeed' will replace the formidable

acronym), once you have a basic understanding of RSS both the power
and the value of the resource become clear very quickly.

URLs mentioned in this chapter

http://209.174.209.6/nashville/library/news.htm

http://30boxes.com

http://allrss.com/rssreaders.html

www.atomenabled.org

www.bloglines.com

www.comicalert.com

http://cybrary.uwinnipeg.ca

www.dailyrotation.com

www.delicious.com

http://demo.planzo.com

http://dir.yahoo.com/Computers_and_Internet/Data_Formats/XML_eXtensible
    _Markup_Language_/RSS/RSS_Readers_and_Aggregators

http://directory.google.com/Top/Reference/Libraries/Library_and_Information_
    Science/Technical_Services/Cataloguing/Metadata/RDF/Applications/RSS/
    News_Readers

www.download.com

www.engineeringvillage2.org

http://era.indecorous.com/email.html

http://eventful.com

http://feed2js.org

www.feeddigest.com

www.feedity.com

www.feedostyle.com

http://feeds.searchengineland.com/searchengineland

www.feedyes.com

www.feedzilla.com

www.flickr.com

www.furl.net

www.google.com/reader

http://grazr.com

www.hipcal.com

www.icerocket.com

http://ieeexplore.ieee.org/xpl/periodicals.jsp

www.ingentaconnect.com/about/researchers/subscribing_to_rss_feeds

www.justtheflight.co.uk/rss/flights.html

www.kickrss.com

www.live.com

www.mailbucket.org

http://monster.com/Monster.com

http://mosuki.com

http://my.detod.com

www.ncbi.nlm.nih.gov/entrez/query.fcgi?DB=pubmed

http://news.bbc.co.uk/shared/bsp/hi/services/htmlsyndication/html/default.
     stm

http://news.google.com

www.newsfeedmaker.com

www.philb.com

www.ponyfish.com

www.proquest.co.uk/syndication/rss

www.r-mail.org

www.rethinkip.com

http://rss.sagepub.com/rss

www.rssauction.com

www.rssmix.com

www.rsspect.com

www.rss-to-javascript.com

www.rssweather.com

http://sophos.com

www.sphere.com

http://syndication.iop.org/?site

www.technorati.com

www.thewebcomiclist.com

www.topix.net

www.virusbtn.com/support/feeds/index.xml

http://web.freepint.com/forum/bar/list.php

http://wiki.wonko.com/software/mailfeed

Chapter 3

Weblogs

Introduction

Weblogs, or blogs for short, were right in the vanguard of Web 2.0 developments, and are good examples of what Web 2.0 means (if we can agree on a definition of course!): they give control to an individual or group; technologically they are easy to use and don't require any great understanding; they are platform independent; and they can be accessed from any online computer regardless of geographical location.

Weblogs should require little by way of introduction since they have been around for the last few years (though their history actually stretches back into the late 1990s) and it's impossible to use the internet without coming across weblogs in one form or another. They are proving very popular, and the increase in the number of weblogs matches the explosion of websites a few years ago, with the evidence from Technorati at **www.technorati.com/weblog/2006/02/81.html** pointing to one new weblog being created every second of the day – over 75,000 a day.

This chapter will provide a little background to weblogs in general terms, although it will not include an in-depth discussion, since there is already a good body of work on the subject. Rather, I will look at ways in which weblogs can be enhanced to provide more information, how they can become useful repositories of data in their own right, and how they can be utilized in conjunction with other resources.

What are weblogs?

Weblogs are often described as online diaries. That is certainly true as far as it goes, but unfortunately that isn't very far at all. Many weblogs are designed simply to act as a way of recording what an individual is doing or thinking at a particular period of time, but those are of little or no interest to us in the present context. A rather more useful way of considering them is to view them as a mechanism where experts in particular subject areas are able to share their knowledge, understanding and opinions with other people, often based on current events or specific or general interest.

We are fortunate that in the information industry there are so many experts who are willing to share their knowledge, experience and information with colleagues, and if you haven't yet explored the world of the weblog I would certainly encourage you to take a peek before you progress further with this chapter. There are a number of resources that

Screen-shot reproduced with permission.

Figure 3.1
The Liszen search interface screen

you can use to kick-start your explorations, and I would suggest taking at look at Liszen at **www.liszen. com** (shown in Figure 3.1) which connects you to over 500 library and library-related weblogs – simply run a search for a subject that interests you, and take a look at some of the posts that people have made on that particular subject area.

While you're there, take a look at the Liszen Trends page at **http:// liszen.com/ trends**, which displays stories in the news that are of interest to information professionals, who are able to rank stories that are of particular interest – a nice way of keeping up to date with what is happening. When you've taken a look at Liszen, move on and explore LibWorm (shown in Figure 3.2) at **www.libworm. com**, which provides access to 1000 library and library-related weblogs, and either run

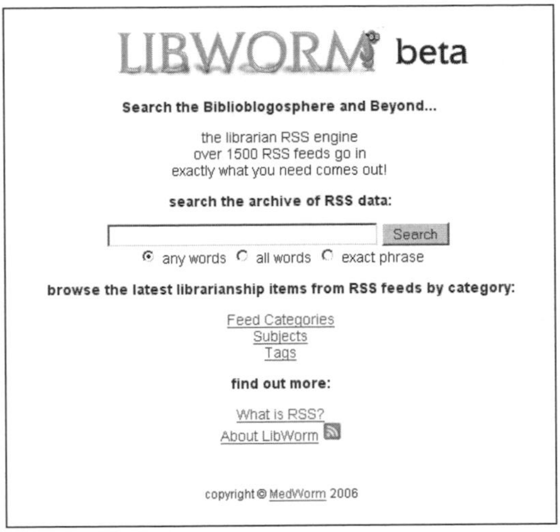

© MedWorm 2006. Screen-shot reproduced with thanks.

Figure 3.2 The LibWorm home page

a search or browse the list of feed categories at **www.libworm.com/rss/ librariancategories.php** or take a look at the subject approach at **www. libworm.com/rss/librarianqueries.php**. Between these resources you should get a better idea of what is available.

While you're reading weblog postings from different people, do, however, keep in mind some of the basic criteria about weblogs. That is to say:

- *Weblogs are personal*
  The people who write weblogs are almost always expressing their own point of view about the subject they're writing about. If the weblog is written in conjunction with an organization you may be reading about the subject based on that organization's point of view. There's nothing wrong with this, of course, but there is an inherent bias – even if it's only based on what the weblog author decides to write about or to ignore!
- *Weblogs are chronological*
  Weblogs usually display the most recent information at the top of the page, and as new items are added they replace the previous latest item, which slips down the list. Older items are then usually archived month by month.

- *Currency is important*
  Weblogs are generally written with the emphasis on the here and now, things that are happening today, or perhaps happened yesterday. If you're looking for older information, or archival data, a weblog isn't going to be of much help. On the other hand, if you are researching current data, or need to keep informed about new and breaking stories and events, weblogs are an important resource to use.
- *Weblogs respond, they don't create*
  That is to say, most weblogs and weblog entries are commenting on what is happening in the news, rather than making it themselves. However, there are always exceptions to this, and increasingly organizations are using weblogs as an adjunct to, or replacement for, traditional press releases. For example, the best way to keep up to date with what Google is doing is to subscribe to its weblogs. (For more information on subscribing to weblogs, please take a look at the previous chapter, on RSS.)
- *There is often an opportunity to collaborate with or respond to the author*
  Many weblogs allow readers to post comments, and these can be a useful resource themselves, as some interesting and valuable discussions can arise out of a particularly thought-provoking weblog entry.
- *The subject is king*
  Most weblogs focus on a particular subject area, be it broad or narrow. However, within that focus many weblogs classify entries into particular subject areas, and it's possible for readers to click on a category and read everything that the author has written on that particular subject.

Searching weblogs

The previous resources, Liszen and LibWorm, specifically focus on the information community, but obviously there will be many times when you want data that relates to other subject areas. There are a lot of search engines that focus on searching weblogs and it's worth using these to identify both weblogs and specific information relating to your search. A few examples are Technorati, at **www.technorati.com**; IceRocket at **www.icerocket.com**; Google Blog search, **http://blogsearch.google.com**; or Ask blogs and feeds, **http://uk.ask.com/?o=312#subject:bls|pg:1**. Alternatively, try a directory listing: Yahoo! has a useful one at **http://dir.yahoo.com/Computers_and_ Internet/Internet/World_Wide_Web/Weblogs**, although it's quite limited in size.

Many of these search engines also allow you to save your search(es) as RSS feeds, as discussed in more detail in the previous chapter, so it's always worth remembering how much of a useful resource they can be.

Creating weblogs

It's very easy to create a weblog for yourself: in fact it's one of the easiest things you can do on the internet, since the whole purpose of weblogging or blogging is to have a place where you can publicize your own opinions, rather than concentrate on the difficulties of writing HTML. Some weblog-authoring tools are commercial in nature, such as TypePad at **www.typepad.com**, which does admittedly provide a lot of functionality for the (small) price, and other types are free, such as Blogger, which is owned by Google and can be found at **www.blogger.com**. Other software is designed to be run on your own system, rather than on the servers of the company providing the authoring tool, such as Moveable Type at **www.movabletype.org**.

Since this chapter isn't really about creating weblogs I suggest that, if you don't already have a weblog yourself, it is worth spending the short amount of time it will take to actually create one for yourself. Don't worry about getting everything perfect to start with, just dive in and start - you can always scrub everything that you've done and start again if necessary. The aforementioned Blogger is a good choice for beginners, as it boasts - quite rightly in my experience - that you can create a weblog in three easy steps, and it won't take you more than five minutes. Alternative packages that you may wish to consider are LiveJournal at **www.livejournal.com** (particularly useful if you want to create a personal weblog), Xanga at **www.xanga.com**, Vox at **www.vox.com** or MySpace at **www.myspace.com**. Other packages are listed in the Wikipedia at **http://en.wikipedia.org/wiki/Weblog_software**.

Using weblogs as an information consumer

Clearly the easiest and most blatantly obvious thing to do with weblogs is to read them! If you have only one or two that interest you, visiting them directly on a regular basis will work perfectly well, although, to be frank, if you have only one or two weblogs that you read regularly you may not have looked hard enough. Once you get beyond a handful then you need to bring in the bigger guns in the form of an RSS reader, which we have already looked at. That way you can keep up to date with what is happening quickly and simply.

Rather than just looking at weblogs on a case-by-case basis, merging or mixing feeds in one format or another, such as KickRSS at **www.kickrss.com**, is a sensible option. This particular resource also allows a user to publish a merged feed for other people to view, either by going directly to the URL or by adding the RSS feed to their own news aggregator such as Bloglines. Consequently it's very easy to set up a series of master feeds, aggregating content from many different sources. This saves a considerable amount of time when it comes to reading material, but more importantly, if you have established a number of these master feeds, you can make them available to your own clients by publishing the RSS stream onto a web page. KickRSS also keeps you informed about the reliability of any particular feed – if it realizes that there have been no new postings for some time, or that it is unable to access a feed it informs the feed owner, who can then investigate matters and if necessary drop the offending feed.

At the risk of repetition, you can add an entire feed to another resource, such as a web page or a start page (discussed in Chapter 5) and create a blended resource. For example, a local history resource could take weblogs and news feeds from local newspapers, organizations, individuals, customized searches and your own weblog, if you write one. Alternatively, instead of a subject-oriented vertical resource like that you might produce a resource that includes weblogs from a number of doctors, or lawyers, irrespective of their particular areas of interest.

Ultimately, weblogs are just a simple, very useful way to keep up to date with what is happening in a subject area, or with a particular individual or organization, and the associated resources such as news aggregators pull the data to you, meaning that you can get on with your job, safe in the knowledge that if you have done your job correctly in the first place, by identifying key individuals and key weblogs in your subject area, you will not miss out on important information.

Using weblogs as an information provider

While simply reading weblogs can be a very exciting, enjoyable and useful way to spend some of your time, the production of a weblog will be all of those things, but increased tenfold – and it can improve your productivity and raise your profile. One very important point, however, before we start to look at what you can do with a weblog in detail, is this – think less in terms of a traditional weblog (indeed, if such a creature even exists), but more in terms of having the ability to produce information that can be repackaged into an almost infinite number of formats, according to your needs and those of your clients. Being able to work with your data in an RSS format means that although the data starts off in one format (the weblog) you can then start to turn it into others quickly and easily, without the requirement for outside assistance or intervention. Moreover, as we shall see shortly, there are an increasing number of resources that can be bolted onto a weblog to turn it from a simple chronologically based utility into something far more detailed and valuable.

Weblogs for promotion and publicity

Whatever you are doing in your library or information centre for your users, then you want people to know about it, or there is little point in doing it. Some of the things that you might want to keep users informed about are:

■ *Opening hours*
Admittedly not the most exciting of things, but an absolute must. This could be broadened out to include other factual information about the service – location and contact details, for example. This can of course go straight onto a web page, but sometimes closures can be unexpected and unplanned, and a weblog entry may well be the quickest and most effective way of getting that information out to

people – particularly if you have your weblog headlines on your web page as well.

■ *New library resources*

There is always a danger when dealing with exciting things such as the internet of forgetting some of the basics, so a weblog that lists new additions to the library – new books, new subscriptions (both paper and electronic) or even new members of staff – will help keep the library towards the forefront of people's minds.

■ *Specific library events*

If you are planning an event within the library, be it an author visit/reading, children's activity, games day, focus on a particular subject, or activity related to a time of the year, it's worth while mentioning in a weblog. Moreover, while the event is actually taking place, why not get a member of staff to blog about it? There may well be people who would like to have attended but are unable to, so at least they can get a flavour of the event. In fact, why stop at getting staff to blog – perhaps you could encourage users to write in their own weblogs and link to them, to get a fully rounded experience? Photograph the event, upload the pictures to a resource such as Flickr at **www.flickr.com** and then incorporate those into the weblog as well.

■ *Encourage debate and interaction*

A weblog can be used very effectively to interact with users. Don't forget that you can offer readers the option of giving their own contributions via the comments field. Have a 'book of the month' posting, either to show people a historical manuscript (something Edinburgh University Library weblog does at **www.lib.ed.ac.uk/ resources/collections/specdivision/botm.shtml**) or to focus on a specific book and seek readers' thoughts and opinions on it.

■ *Create a virtual exhibition*

Have a weblog that concentrates on a particular library resource, such as a series of historical books or artifacts. Take photographs, post them to Flickr, use the weblog to link to other resources on the internet, include comments from visitors, and tie the weblog version into a 'real life' version of the same thing. Instead of having those visitors signing a paper guestbook, perhaps involve them by asking them to leave comments on the weblog. Of course, some of this could be done with a straightforward web page, but it may well be easier and quicker to do this using weblog software, and without having to wait until the overworked technical support team can offer assistance and encouragement in their usual fashion.

■ *Involve staff and users*
Encourage staff to contribute to the weblog(s): not only will that give them a stake in the resource, but it will also give readers an opportunity to get to know members of staff a little more as 'real people' rather than semi-anonymous individuals. At the other end of the spectrum, if you have particularly enthusiastic users, or people who have made a real contribution to the library, write a post about them, or have them do it. Weblogs are a great way of reaching out to users and getting their involvement in a far simpler and easier way than any other method. You can create different weblogs for different user groups, which is particularly useful if you run a service for different groups, such as teenagers and senior citizens, or lawyers and researchers.

Weblogs for information

Another obvious reason for having a weblog is to bring information quickly and easily to the attention of your readership. In the old paradigm of the provision of information it would have been necessary to take the data and either create a new web page to contain the information, or to incorporate it into an existing page. This would have meant writing the appropriate coding for the page (and getting it correct!), and then uploading the information, and perhaps waiting for the search engines to index the new data, or to wait and hope that your visitors will return at some unspecified time in the future. However, with a weblog, once you are aware of the information you wish to make available, it's a question of writing a post, adding it to the weblog 'pinging' various resources (that is to say, informing weblog search engines that you have new information and getting them to come and index it) and carrying on with whatever you were doing.

Categorization

Some weblog-authoring packages make this much easier than others. Some tools allow you to create categories, and when a post is added to the weblog it can be assigned to one or several different categories. This makes it much easier to find information in the future, since a click on a category will retrieve all of the appropriate postings. This solution is good if you wish to maintain only one weblog. On the other hand, if you have subject specialists in the organization it may make more sense to have a small number of weblogs dealing with particular subject areas. Neither is the 'right' approach – it all depends on what you wish to achieve.

This category approach is one of the first examples of the way in which a weblog can be used as a repository of information: the weblog can be used as a place to store information on, and links to, a huge number of resources. The ease of use of a weblog makes it an attractive alternative to creating a web page on a site to do exactly the same thing, and with the addition of an RSS feed it's an excellent way in which people can keep up to date. Moreover, if the weblog is one that supports multiple authors (and not all do, so it's worth checking if this is something that appeals to you), as soon as one colleague or friend has found something and blogged it, everyone knows about it.

Figure 3.3
The Eurekster Swicki hosted on the UKeIG weblog

Searching

However, we need not stop at that point. Chapter 7 looks in some detail at the concept of building your own search engine (which is a slight misnomer, since you create a subset of sites and pages indexed by a search engine as your search 'universe'), and such an engine can be included on a weblog page. There are several resources that can do this, such as the Eurekster Swicki, found at **http://swicki. eurekster.com**: an example of it in practice can be seen on the UKeIG (the UK eInformation Group) weblog at **www.ukeig.org.uk/blog** and in Figure 3.3.

Similar resources are available from traditional search engines such as Google and Yahoo!, and from other companies as well, and these are covered in more depth in Chapter 7. The important point here is that the weblog can start to reflect the interests of its readership, not just of the author(s), given that the results displayed for any search are based in part on previous searches that other people have run. It also means that readers do not actually have to leave the weblog page to run a search, which is a benefit for them.

Linking

Any weblog software will allow you to have links to other sites, so you can use that functionality to connect to other key sites that cover the subject area that the weblog concentrates on. This is often a 'blogroll' which lists other weblogs that the author reads, but there is no particular reason why this need be the case – they can link to anywhere that has a URL! In fact, you could decide to link to various pages on your own website, perhaps ones that include RSS feeds, so the weblog becomes the central point, or trunk, with the web pages as branches and the feeds as leaves. At this point the arboreal metaphor is beginning to get a little excessive, but I'm sure you get the idea.

Weblogs and RSS

RSS feeds, as well as being hosted on web pages, can also be incorporated into a weblog sidebar. It's not going to be possible to mention everything of interest in a weblog, but at the same time you do want to be able to give your readers as much information as possible and appropriate. Consider creating a search with one of the search engines that will return data in an RSS format, or from BBC news feeds for example, and have that in the sidebar of the weblog. Not only are your users benefiting from your skill and experience as a researcher, you can provide them with an in-depth focus on specific stories.

Of course there is always the danger of information overload, and while weblogs and RSS feeds were once thought of as a way to reduce this problem, they have actually escalated it to an entirely new level. Tailrank at **http://tailrank.com** is a resource that allows you to provide it with a collection of your feeds in OPML format (your news aggregator should allow you to export your entire collection in this format), and it can then rearrange the data in a newly ranked format with the most important stories at the top of the listing, with the less discussed stories further down. As you might expect, this re-ranked and filtered collection of stories culled from various RSS feeds can itself be exported as an RSS feed (at this point I have visions of cartoons in which the vacuum cleaner sucks up everything, including itself – only with RSS instead) and this could be added to a weblog page as a single feed instead of multiple ones.

Reading lists

A weblog could also include a reading list. Various modules are available (depending on the weblog authoring software) that allow authors to plug in details of the books they are reading: there is an example of how this works with TypePad in my own weblog at **www.philbradley.typepad. com**. This links directly into Amazon, so interested parties can go directly to the book for more information. While this was obviously done for personal use, it would be easy to use the function to create a list of recommended books for a particular subject area or course, perhaps. Within a public library environment the book or books chosen could be those that a book-reading circle or club is in the process of exploring.

Photographs

There is no need to stop at books either: a weblog does not have to be limited to text, so it may be appropriate to include photographs. These could either be incorporated directly into a weblog posting (Flickr, discussed in Chapter 10, supports this easily), or with a collection of photographs in a sidebar, or as a link to another collection hosted by the authoring-software creators. This would be an excellent repository of photographs taken at a specific event, for example, or it could contain photographs of members of staff, or a photographic tour of the library, or humorous signs – the possibilities are almost endless.

Podcasts

It is also possible to give your weblog a real voice by including podcasts. Chapter 4 covers these in detail but, put briefly, a podcast is an audio recording: it could be someone reading out a weblog entry, someone singing a song, a guided tour – just about anything at all. An increasing number of resources allow users to add weblog entries by voice – and although at the moment this appears to be limited to the USA, I'm sure this will not be the case for long. One product that offered this service was Audioblogger, but it has recently died (an unfortunate outcome of many Web 2.0 projects). It has been replaced with various other options, such as Gabcast at **http://gabcast. com**, Hipcast at **www.hipcast.com** and Gcast at **www.gcast.com**.

While in some respects this might just be considered to be a 'cool' thing to do, adding podcast-like or voice recordings of events would give readers (and I suppose we should also now say listeners) a real feeling of inclusion, especially if it includes a quick 'hello' from an author if you're recording information on an author reading, or various children adding their own comments on an event that the library has created for them.

Video and other resources

Using some of the resources available at Widgetbox at **www.widgetbox. com** readers could be kept up to date via your favourite radio station or music chart, or you can even go to the next level by including video clips. Obviously the times when this would be appropriate would depend very much on the particular reason for the weblog, but it's not something that should necessarily be ruled out.

It's always worth keeping a lookout to see if any new resources have been launched onto the market that will allow you to incorporate something new into a weblog. For example, SlideShare at **www.slideshare.net** is a case in point. It is basically a resource that allows users to upload, store and share PowerPoint presentations. The Web 2.0 element enters the story in that it's possible for other people to add comments on a slideshow or individual slide, and there is a very simple cut-and-paste option that allows people to add the slideshow to a web page or a weblog. Figure 3.4 (overleaf) shows this in action on my own weblog – while the position and placement isn't perfect, it does the intended job.

As a result it wouldn't be difficult to create either a weblog or a category for presentations, or for training, or orientation, for example. Once the original presentation has been created it simply needs to be uploaded to

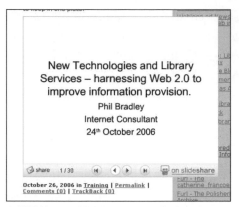

New Technologies and Library
Services – harnessing Web 2.0 to
improve information provision.
Phil Bradley
Internet Consultant
24th October 2006

Figure 3.4
Embedding a PowerPoint slideshow into a weblog

SlideShare, the code to embed the presentation into another resource is cut and pasted, and then it is simply added into a new weblog entry. This is quick and easy: an excellent way of making data available in a different format, with nothing stored on your own servers or system, and with no need to get a single technician involved! This would also work nicely if you wanted to create a slightly different type of event record – instead of saving photographs to Flickr, simply pop them into the presentation and provide a quick slide-show in a limited amount of space.

Other links

There may be times when you feel that it's important to keep people on your weblog, but want to point them towards other resources as well, in slightly more depth than simply by linking. This is where a product called Bitty Browser at **www.bitty.com** becomes useful (see also p. 184). It's like having a browser window permanently installed on a web page – although admittedly a rather small window. It's also possible to set the resource to pre-load content from a specific site or indeed news feed. This would again be very useful if you wanted to have a training element to a weblog, since it would be possible to write an entry discussing a particular subject or concept, and then have a link to a site that demonstrated it – without confusing the viewer or losing them for good when they go off to explore another site in more detail.

More audience participation

Another way of encouraging audience participation within the weblog environment is to add a chat box facility or to get involved with instant messaging. These are discussed in more detail in Chapter 9, but there are many resources, such as Gabbly at **http://gabbly.com** or Shoutbox at **www.widgetbox.com/widget/shoutbox**, which work on a simple cut-and-paste basis and provide the basics of chat. One of these could either be incorporated into a weblog sidebar as a general resource for visitors and weblog authors alike, or it could be embedded into a weblog posting as part of a specific event or a Friday afternoon 'ask the librarian' session.

Introducing a weblog into the working environment

As you've seen, there is a great deal that can be done with weblogs in a library environment, and it is very easy to just go out and create one. The software is available, the webspace is free and I'm sure there are ideas aplenty. It's very tempting since, in the words of the sportswear company, you can 'just do it'. However, there are also dangers inherent in that approach, and some things that are worth considering.

If you create a weblog for your library or wider organization, whose 'voice' is being heard? Is it your personal voice, the voice of the position that you hold, the voice of the library or indeed the voice of the entire organization? If you write a weblog that protests against a particular piece of legislation that may well be perfectly acceptable on a personal weblog, but your employer may be less than happy if the organization is perceived to be criticizing the government. Consequently you need to spend time discussing with people in your organization exactly what boundaries exist for the weblog(s).

Who is responsible for saying what, and when? This latter issue is also very important: in the days before the instant nature of weblogs it was possible to spend a reasonable amount of time discussing an issue before making a statement on it. However, given the nature of blogging, where speed does sometimes appear to be the most important element in the process, a clear chain of communication and command needs to be established so that the right person can respond quickly and effectively.

The weblog(s) should make it quite clear right from the outset that the bloggers are speaking in a personal capacity, or on behalf of the organization, or whatever it may be, simply so that readers will be clear on that point right at the start. The writers themselves need to understand where their responsibilities lie and, tempting though it may be to stray, they should keep within their own boundaries. It's also necessary to be aware of what is or is not confidential to the company or organization. While interesting news stories may circulate within the four walls of the building, that doesn't necessarily mean they can be discussed externally.

Accuracy, respect, integrity and honesty are key ingredients in a successful weblog strategy. Weblogs are very powerful tools – they wouldn't have become so successful so quickly if they weren't – but with that power comes a certain amount of danger, and the wrong thing said in a weblog can be disseminated with frightening speed. There have been a few instances with official Google weblogs when staff posted material that shouldn't have been included. While these were honest mistakes, they did raise eyebrows among Google-watchers throughout the world.

It is only sensible therefore to be clear within all levels of the organization exactly where individual levels of responsibility lie with respect to weblogs, and setting up such a policy is almost certainly going to take considerably longer than actually creating the weblog.

Conclusion

As this chapter has demonstrated, a weblog is considerably more than 'an online diary' – with the addition of bolt-on utilities and resources and ease of use, a weblog is increasingly becoming a destination site in its own right. Weblogs are, and always will be, mainly reflective of one individual 'voice', be it that of a single author or a small group of authors working together, but having value-added information with pointers to other information makes their use quite compelling.

Added to this of course is the dual nature of the weblog – not only is it an excellent method of getting current information quickly with minimal fuss, but it is a superb way of making it available. The more that someone uses or reads weblogs, the more I suspect that they will be able to see ways in which they too can contribute to that dreadful, but descriptive, term, 'the blogosphere'.

URLs mentioned in this chapter

www.bitty.com

www.blogger.com

http://blogsearch.google.com

http://dir.yahoo.com/Computers_and_Internet/Internet/World_Wide_Web/
    Weblogs

http://en.wikipedia.org/wiki/Weblog_software

www.flickr.com

http://gabbly.com

http://gabcast.com

www.gcast.com

www.hipcast.com

www.icerocket.com

www.kickrss.com

www.lib.ed.ac.uk/resources/collections/specdivision/botm.shtml

www.libworm.com

www.libworm.com/rss/librariancategories.php

www.libworm.com/rss/librarianqueries.php

www.liszen.com

http://liszen.com/trends

www.livejournal.com

www.movabletype.org/

www.myspace.com

www.philbradley.typepad.com

www.slideshare.net

http://swicki.eurekster.com

http://tailrank.com

www.technorati.com

www.technorati.com/weblog/2006/02/81.html

www.typepad.com

http://uk.ask.com/?o=312#subject:bls|pg:1

www.ukeig.org.uk/blog

www.vox.com

www.widgetbox.com

www.widgetbox.com/widget/shoutbox

www.xanga.com

Chapter 4

Finding your voice – using podcasts

Introduction

Text is a wonderful medium within which to provide content: it sits quite happily on a page waiting to be read, digested, understood and acted upon. We rely on textual information in one format or another to provide us with data all of the time – I, as writer of this book, and you, as reader, don't need to have this discussion. we both already know. However, text has its own drawbacks, not least of which is the fact that unless the words can be placed into context they can mean different things. I was at a conference recently and used a slide that said 'I don't care' on it. This was then reported by a well-known blogger, and someone else then picked up on it and assumed that I'd meant something completely different from what I had actually said. Of course, they could have checked with me directly, because without the tone and context the words by themselves were almost useless. How different that situation would have been if my voice could have been heard, with the appropriate nuances – it would have been obvious that far from not caring, I did care a great deal.

This is of course where podcasts come into play – the ability to record one's voice to much more accurately describe something. This chapter looks at exactly what podcasting is, how it works and the ways in which libraries are using it.

What is a podcast?

A podcast is simply the name given to a file that is a voice recording for playback on a computer, or saved onto an MP3 digital audio player and listened to at some future point. The name comes from the activity of broadcasting and listening to the file on an Apple iPod player, and was used in an article in *The Guardian* newspaper as a synonym for the rather clumsy 'audioblogging'. The full story is at **http://technology.guardian. co.uk/weekly/story/0,16376,1683937,00.html**.

The host, author or voice of the podcast is often known, unsurprisingly, as a podcaster, and the delivery mechanism as podcasting. There are obviously other audio formats available, however, and podcasts differ in that they can be downloaded automatically using RSS software and played immediately there and then. This is not really the place to go into the history or early development of podcasting, but interested readers may wish to consult the appropriate Wikipedia article at **http://en.wikipedia. org/wiki/History_of_podcasting**. However, it is worth pointing out that podcasting has become very popular very quickly – on 28 September 2004 there were 24 hits with Google for the term 'podcasts', 526 hits two days later and then over 100,000 by October that same year. In October 2006 the same search returned over 153 million results.

Why are podcasts so popular?

Podcasts and podcasting have become popular for a wide variety of reasons, not least of which is that a podcast is simple to create, as we shall see. It is a very convenient way of providing access to data – a podcast can be listened to on a computer while the listener is also busy doing something else on their machine. Alternatively it can be stored, copied onto an MP3 player and listened to while jogging, on the bus – almost anywhere in fact. Podcasts are created by a wide variety of individuals, from politicians to comedians; they have been adopted by mainstream broadcasters such as the BBC and radio stations around the world; and they have been used by print media (such as *Nature* magazine) to supplement their printed content. Podcasts have become so popular so quickly that the *New Oxford American Dictionary* declared 'podcasting' as the word of the year for 2005.

Finding and using podcasts

Podcasts, as may reasonably be expected, can be a valuable source of information – if they can be found. There are a number of search engines that can be used to locate podcasts of interest.

Yahoo! Podcasts

Yahoo! Podcasts at **http://podcasts.yahoo.com** is very straightforward to use, as you would expect from one of the leading search engines. A search for 'librarian' resulted in a total of 280 results for both series and episodes, a series being an ongoing collection of podcasts (think radio series) and an episode being a mention in passing in another podcast. Yahoo! indexes both the description of a podcast and any associated tags. Podcasts can be listened to immediately just by clicking on the appropriate link, and Yahoo! will work with your existing software to open the file and allow you to listen to it immediately or to download it for later. In many instances it is also possible to subscribe to a series, and providing the right software is available (such as Apple iTunes, for example) the next episode can be downloaded and placed on the MP3 player the next time it is synchronized with the PC.

Singingfish

Singingfish at **http://search.singingfish.com/sfw/home.jsp** provides access to video and audio material, so it's necessary to limit your search to the audio option if you wish to focus on podcasts. My 'librarian' search returned 188 hits, but some of these were musical items, and adding 'podcast' into the search reduced the results to one, so it was not as useful as the Yahoo! offering.

Podzinger

Podzinger at **http://podzinger.com** provided over 800 hits on my keyword search and very usefully provided a textual excerpt from the podcast when the word was mentioned. This obviously allows for a much more focused search, with greater accuracy. This search engine does have specific software requirements in order for users to listen to podcasts (at the time of writing this was Flash Player 9.0.16+, but it can be downloaded from links on the site).

Blogdigger

Blogdigger is a general weblog search engine, but it does have a media tab, and this can be further refined to audio at **www.blogdigger.com/ media/index.html**. It is very simple and straightforward to use, and the 'librarian' search returned 81 results, although one or two of these were pornographic in nature, so some discretion is advised. Various options were available to allow for downloading or streaming directly to the computer, depending on the file chosen.

There are of course many others that you may wish to try as well as those listed above, such as Podscope at **www.podscope.com**, Podcast.net at **www.podcast.net**, the PodcastDirectory at **www.podcastdirectory.com** and the Podcast Network at **www.thepodcastnetwork.com**. If that still isn't enough, a search using your preferred search engine for 'podcast search engine' will turn up more offerings.

Once you have found a podcast that you wish to listen to you may well find that it is as simple as clicking on a link given on the web page that lists it. Your computer software then takes charge and will play the file for you, and you will be free to pause the file, rewind or move forward, just as though it was an old-fashioned cassette tape. You may wish to subscribe to the various podcasts you find (if that option is available), in which case they will automatically be downloaded for you ready to be copied onto your player when you next synch it. Juice at **http://juicereceiver. sourceforge.net/index.php** is a free cross-platform piece of software that allows you to do exactly that. Alternatively you may simply choose to save the file and copy it across to the MP3 player in exactly the same way that you would do with any other audio file.

Creating podcasts

The creation of a podcast is almost as simple and straightforward as listening to one, and hardly requires any more hardware or software. The important point here is not so much the technical aspects of creating a podcast, but the practicality of content. At first this may appear to be the easy aspect: after all, you have something you wish to say, so surely it's just a matter of saying it? This is unfortunately seldom the case. What may seem to be a light-hearted chat when you play it in your mind can quickly degenerate into a series of 'umms' and 'ahhs', coughs and splutters, with background noise getting in on the act as well. While extemporizing may seem to be the best plan, even experienced speakers can become hypnotized when looking at the microphone, leading to a poor recording. It may then appear to be sensible to write out the entire content and then read it from the page directly into the microphone. Unfortunately that can lead to a very flat, boring delivery – if your audience is in danger of dropping off it's unlikely that they will be taking much notice of what you are trying to say, and more importantly they will not return for another episode.

Each podcaster needs to find his or her own voice, and to work out what works and what does not – there is no overall ten-stage plan to perfect podcasting. In my experience it makes sense to think through the content you wish to include, decide on the order of the different points and perhaps jot down some specific notes that you want included, and then try a dry run-though before recording it properly. Luckily most software will allow you to edit out the inevitable cough or extended pause very easily. The podcast can be of any length of course, and if you have already experimented with a few of the search engines previously mentioned you will have found some podcasts that last for an hour or more, but these tend to be the province of experienced or professional broadcasters and are not something to be emulated by mere mortals such as you and I. It may be best to start with a short podcast of no more than ten minutes' duration Don't forget that the podcast does not need to be a solo activity, and indeed it may make for more interest (and less pressure) if two people can be involved, perhaps with one taking the part of an interviewer and the other answering questions – depending on content of course.

The hardware required

One of the nice things about a lot of Web 2.0 activities is that they do not require any great financial outlay. A microphone may well have been included as part of the bundle that came with the computer. If not, microphones are not expensive to buy, and certainly a product that costs $20 or £10 will be more than adequate to start with: headphone/ microphone combinations of double that cost will also filter out background noise for you. If you intend to start podcasting seriously you may wish to spend more money, but equally until you know if podcasting is for you or your library it's silly to waste money. I would, however, advise against any internal microphones that come with the computer or laptop since they really will not be up to the job.

The software required

As you would expect, there is a lot of software available to assist in the creation of the podcast. One of the most popular packages is Audacity, available free from **http://audacity.sourceforge.net**. This software is multi-platform and has become the standard tool used by podcasters since it allows users to quickly and easily edit content, and to add other sound files (such as intro and outro music). It does have the disadvantage that it cannot easily be used to record conversations with people who are not in the same room, so if you are considering doing telephone interviews you will need to look elsewhere for software. Once the software has been downloaded and installed and the microphone plugged in, it's a straightforward matter to start to record the podcast – Figure 4.1 shows this in operation.

The Audacity software is flexible enough to allow users to listen to the finished article at their leisure and to delete any unwanted clicks or coughs by highlighting the section and then deleting it. Once the podcast is complete you may consider adding a brief jingle at the beginning fading out and one at the end fading in for an extra touch; a site that provides royalty-free music is Flash Kit at **www.flashkit.com/loops**, with over 7000 loops to choose from.

Finally the podcast needs to be saved into an appropriate file format, such as .mp3, and for this one final piece of software the LAME MP3 encoder is needed; details on downloading and installing it can be found at **http://audacity.sourceforge.net/help/faq?s=install&item= lame-mp3**.

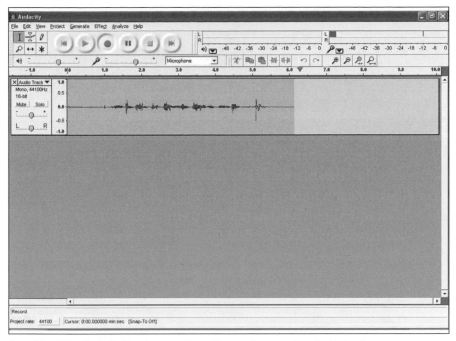

Figure 4.1 The Audacity software beginning to record a podcast

Publishing your podcast

Once the podcast has been saved it needs to be made available for people to listen to. This is also straightforward, and lots of sites will be happy to host the podcast for you, sometimes for free, sometimes for a small fee. Ourmedia at **www.ourmedia.org** is one example, and Odeo at **http://odeo.com** is another resource that will assist you. Alternatively you may decide to simply upload the file to an FTP (file transfer protocol) server and link to it, if you want to make the file available on a website for example, and both Ourmedia and Odeo can make the process of including the podcast into an RSS feed very simple. Once the podcast is up and running, consider submitting the link to podcast directories and resources as mentioned earlier to bring it to the attention of a wider audience.

This is by necessity a quick overview of the process of creating a podcast. More in-depth tutorials are available on the web: a particularly helpful one is 'Create your own podcast' by Rick Broida at **http://reviews.**

cnet.com/4520-11293_7-6246557-1.html?tag=bnav, and another is 'Beginner's guide to podcasting' by Kirk McElhearn at www.ilounge.com/ index.php/articles/comments/beginners-guide-to-podcast-creation. I hope the foregoing explanation will encourage readers who were interested but thought it would be too difficult to actually have a go themselves.

Using podcasts in a library environment

The most obvious way of using a podcast within a library environment is to create a library guide that new employees or students can download and use. The podcast can 'walk' them around the library in much the same way as that a more traditional human guide would do. Of course, this lacks the personal touch (though listeners can always be encouraged to ask questions of nearby library staff), but on the other hand it does result in much less noise and disruption to other users of the library. Library tours are becoming much more common, particularly within academic environments, and they bring many benefits with them, as the case study below illustrates.

However, it would be a shame to simply limit the use of a podcast to a library guide:

■ Separate tours could be created to focus on particular subject collections, for example, or to provide overviews of particular resources.
■ Short instructional guides could be created to assist users in learning the basics of particular pieces of software or hardware, for example.
■ Weekly podcasts could be created to keep library users up to date with new additions to the library.
■ Events can be captured on a podcast, such as an author reading, for example, or recollections of times long gone as part of a local history project. It's important to remember that a podcast is not restricted by geography or tied to a computer, so someone could make a digital recording of an event, or report on it and then cut and paste parts of that into a podcast.
■ Members of staff can be interviewed: a fun way to introduce a new member of the team and to make them part of the organization

might be to have a more experienced colleague do a brief recorded interview, by way of introduction, and finding out a little more about them.

- Library users can be involved in the creation of podcasts by getting them to engage in a question-and-answer session with the head of library services, which can be recorded and made available as a podcast.
- Staff may be able to record a conference for use in a podcast.
- Public libraries can further engage with their local communities by becoming involved in events and archiving them in the form of podcasts.
- Enthusiastic students can be marvellous ambassadors for a library service: music students can be encouraged to get involved with podcasts by getting them to create appropriate intro loops, journalism students can record interesting articles and items for inclusion in a weekly podcast, literature students can do book reviews – the list really is endless.

Of course, podcasts do not need to be used or listened to in isolation: there is no reason why they should not be used alongside other resources. For example, a podcast could be used in conjunction with a PowerPoint presentation to enhance a learning experience. A web page could be created for a podcast and links made available on the page so that the listener could click on these at specific times during the podcast to look at the site being discussed, or view the image being referred to.

Legal issues

Inevitably there are legal issues related to the whole area of podcasting – not least because a podcast is a creative work. This is not a great problem if only one person creates the podcast, but once two or more people become involved, with perhaps snippets of music from third parties and so on, it can get more complex very quickly. Clearly this is made even more difficult because podcasting is a new medium, but a lot of existing laws cover the area. Given that I do not come from a legal background, it would be inappropriate for me to pass comment on the legalities of podcasting in specific instances, and readers are advised to visit the Podcasting Legal Guide, published by the Creative Commons at **http://wiki.creativecommons.org/Podcasting_Legal_Guide**, for more in-depth discussion.

 ## Case study: The use of podcasts in a library

The James Joyce Library in University College Dublin (UCD) is a large multi-level library which has introduced a podcast tour of the library for new users. Diarmuid Stokes (Branch Librarian for the veterinary medicine library) was kind enough to spend some time with me to explain exactly how this was done.

Q: Can you tell me a little bit about the library first of all, to put it into context – number of staff, students, books, size and so on.
A: University College Dublin is the largest academic institution in Ireland, with approximately 22,000 students. The UCD Library is the largest open-access library in Ireland, containing over one million volumes. The James Joyce Library is on the main campus and is spread over four levels.
Q: Why did you decide to create an audio tour?
A: The James Joyce Library is a large multi-level library and students, especially at the start of the academic year, can find it difficult to find their way around. There had been an old audio cassette tour, which had become out of date and was not being used any more. Josh Clark [Liaison Librarian for the physical sciences] and I made a proposal to Carmel O'Sullivan, Associate Librarian (Resources & Information), about updating the tour and making it more accessible to students.
Q: Did you need to get permission from anyone, or was it just a case of 'go for it'?
A: UCD Library is putting a lot of effort into the development of information skills training and user education, and this all

needs to be co-ordinated. We felt that the tour would fit into this general area and so we made a proposal to management, but when we received their support it was very much a case of 'go for it'.

Q: What specific advantages do you think it provides, and are there any disadvantages?

A: Being available on the web it means that the students can access it wherever they want. It has the potential of lowering the staffing resources associated with giving tours. It also means that new users of the library are not restrained by the availability of staff to show them around the facility.

Q: What software and hardware did you use?

A: We used an iMac laptop with Garageband software (**www.apple.com/ilife/garageband**) and iTunes (**www.apple.com/itunes**). We also had to purchase a good-quality microphone and an amplifier, and to get it all to work together. Once the tour was created we then used Dreamweaver to upload the tour to the library website.

Q: Did you need to get your technical staff involved? What was their attitude towards the project?

A: We didn't need to get our systems staff involved. Josh and I are both on the library's website development group and have a certain level of technical knowledge. Using an i-Mac and the Garageband software helped, as they are designed to be user-friendly and tolerant of the beginner.

We did have problems with the actual recording of the tour, as neither of us had any experience in this area. We were very lucky to have had the assistance of Dr Richard Arnett from the School of Agriculture, Food Science & Veterinary Medicine. Richard had developed a series of veterinary-medicine-related podcasts and was kind enough to demonstrate basic recording techniques to us.

Q: Was it difficult to create the podcast? Did you make many mistakes? What would you do differently next time?

A: It wasn't too difficult. The hardest part was coming up

with the script. Developing a route around the library and
putting oneself in the shoes of a new user of the library
meant looking at the library anew. We had to forget the
geography of the building that we know well, and break the
tour into easily understandable (we hope) chunks.

We recruited two staff members to be the 'voices of the
Library' (each person took two floors), and sometimes had to
do numerous takes to get the right sound levels. To ensure
that we were intelligible we tested the tour on new members
of staff and then amended the tour based on their feedback.

Q: How have you publicized the resource?

A: The tour was publicized on the library website
(**www.ucd.ie/library**) and on the UCD Science blog
(**http://ucdscience.blogspot.com**). We also placed posters at
the library entrance and on all of the library's information
desks. The library recently placed a large plasma screen at
the entrance to advertise various library services and we had
a presence there as well.

**Q: What sort of feedback have you had from management,
staff and users?**

A: Unfortunately, due to technical difficulties, we didn't
launch the tour at the start of the year as planned. This delay
meant that quite a lot of the usual library-user education, i.e.
tours, had already happened. As a result, much of the
potential audience didn't require the tour. Unfortunately this
has meant that feedback from users has been lacking.

Feedback from management and staff has been very
encouraging and appreciative.

**Q: Are there any plans to provide library users with more
library podcasts?**

A: Now that we know how to create a podcast we are
beginning to think about other podcasts. Being in Ireland, we
are thinking about an Irish-language tour. We also have
students from many different countries, so providing tours in
those languages is also a possibility.

Q: What are you thinking of doing next?

A: We are thinking of creating podcasts that explain various library services such as interlibrary loans, or how the book-ordering system works, or involving particular subject information desk staff. We might try this in interview format, which is something we have heard done in other libraries (mostly in the USA).

Q: Are there any 'words of wisdom' that you'd pass on to other libraries considering creating their own audio tour?

A: Know the technology! Also be prepared to put in more time and effort than you might think, and prepare to learn more about your library, or at least prepare to see it from a different perspective – your user's.

Conclusion

At first, podcasts may appear to be a difficult technology to come to grips with, but in actual fact the technology is in many ways the easiest part of the whole experience. Putting together the 'story', and getting used to being recorded, is likely to be the more challenging element of the exercise.

A podcast is a great way of introducing the library or information service to groups of people, and of reminding them that you're available, and can provide them with information even if they don't come to the library.

URLs mentioned in this chapter

www.apple.com/ilife/garageband

www.apple.com/itunes

http://audacity.sourceforge.net

http://audacity.sourceforge.net/help/faq?s=install&item=lame-mp3

www.blogdigger.com/media/index.html

http://en.wikipedia.org/wiki/History_of_podcasting

www.flashkit.com/loops

www.ilounge.com/index.php/articles/comments/beginners-guide-to-
podcast-creation

http://juicereceiver.sourceforge.net/index.php

http://odeo.com

www.ourmedia.org

www.podcast.net

www.podcastdirectory.com

http://podcasts.yahoo.com

www.podscope.com

http://podzinger.com

http://reviews.cnet.com/4520-11293_7-6246557-1.html?tag=bnav

http://search.singingfish.com/sfw/home.jsp

http://technology.guardian.co.uk/weekly/story/0,16376,1683937,00.html

www.thepodcastnetwork.com

www.ucd.ie/library

http://ucdscience.blogspot.com

http://wiki.creativecommons.org/Podcasting_Legal_Guide

Chapter 5

Start pages

Introduction

The 'home page' or 'start page' of your browser – and it doesn't matter if it's Firefox, Internet Explorer, Opera or any other – is the one page that you're going to see more often than any other. There are many different types of start page (by that I mean the page that automatically loads whenever you start your browser), and the vast majority of them are a complete waste of time and effort. Commonly a start page will direct the browser to the company that sold you or your organization the computer you're using. Sometimes it will lead into the browser's own site, or that of a search engine or other affiliate you have a relationship with. At other times the start page will be the home page of your own organization, be it company, college or school. If you're slightly more fortunate it may be your own intranet, in which case you might get quicker access to the pages that you're actually interested in.

When I visit libraries or organizations I'm always interested to see exactly where I get taken when the browser starts for the first time, and invariably I'm disappointed, because the page is either one that I'm familiar with, such as Google, or it will be the organization's website, which in most cases will be of little interest to me since I will have already looked at it while researching it. Admittedly, having a search engine load up is quite helpful because there's a fairly high likelihood that I'll want to run a search for something. However, that isn't a foregone conclusion. There are a number of different things that I may want to use when I start the browser up.

1   *E-mail* I check my e-mail on a fairly regular basis, and since I have several accounts, depending on whether the e-mail is personal, for work, a 'catch all' account, or for registration details, there is no guarantee as to which I'll want or need to check first. Most of my e-mail is automatically sent to my Outlook account via my internet service provider, but Gmail, Hotmail and Yahoo! accounts all require attention now and then.

2   *News sites* Being something of a news junkie, as it seems that most people who regularly use the internet are, there are a variety of news sites that I look at, and these differ according to both the time of day and the nature of the news that I'm interested in. I also like to know what the weather is like – and not always in the place that I physically happen to be in!

3   *Weblogs* I read a lot of weblogs, as you'll be aware if you've read Chapter 3, but I can access most of these from my news reader – but I still need to get access to the news reader!

4   *Updating services* I have a variety of alerts set up with search engines such as Technorati and IceRocket to update me on various issues. I could of course add them to my news reader, but many of these alerts are ones that I want only for a very short period of time, perhaps only one or two days while I'm researching a particular project, and there is little point in taking even the few moments that it would take to set them up in Bloglines.

5   *Top links* Most frequent internet users have a number of pages that they look at on a regular basis – 'doing the rounds', as it were, to catch up on what's happening in a favourite forum, or just to see what new jokes have been added to a page. All of these sites need to be remembered or the URLs stored in some way to allow quick and easy access.

6   *Search engines* Sometimes, of course, it is necessary to search, but while we all have favourite search engines that we use as a default there are

others that we use depending on the type of query – looking for images, for example, or checking video, or indeed we may just want to double-check the results of a search. Ready access to several different engines is useful, to say the least.

7 *Quick games* Not everything that we do on the internet is going to be serious of course – very far from it. Many of us have favourite games that we enjoy playing, but once again it can be tiresome to have to remember the page details, browse to it and then start to play. Slightly less game-orientated, but still in the leisure area, it can be enjoyable to read a quote of the day, or play a game to check your vocabulary.

8 *Other utilities* There are other functions on the computer that we find useful – using a calculator, tracking packages, checking the spelling of words, leaving notes for ourselves, creating to-do lists, or checking the time in different locations around the world.

Some of these are certainly quite easy to do with a computer without too much trouble, but some of them are a little more convoluted to do easily and quickly. An obvious resource offered directly by the browser is to make use of the 'Bookmark' or 'Favorite' option. It's not hard to create a folder of 'often visited sites' in order to cover visiting those top links, for example, but this will not help for most of the other things that I want to be able to do. Some of those activities I can do by utilizing specific resources like a pages-watching service (such as WatchThatPage at **www.watchthatpage.com**), which will alert me to recently changed pages, or I can get my RSS aggregator to pull down data for me regularly. However, while these are helpful I still have to do a lot of different things with different resources, and although I'm saving some time it still isn't an ideal solution.

Another solution, which addresses most, though not all, of the points that I've already mentioned, is to use a start page I created myself, and indeed this is something that I did for several years. A basic knowledge of HTML is needed in order to create the initial page, and it can then be stored on the local computer and used as the default home page. It's not too difficult to change – just call up the HTML authoring package, make the change(s) necessary, save the page and the job is finished. However, there are still problems with this approach, not least that if you don't know how to write a basic page it can appear to be a very daunting proposition. Even if you can do this, making changes to pages can be tiresome, and without a rather more advanced knowledge of HTML it's going to be harder to include more complex or interesting functionality as outlined previously. Finally, even if all of these challenges are overcome the start page is residing only on one particular computer. If you use several computers (at home, at work, perhaps at an internet café, maybe a laptop as well) it will be necessary to copy the page to those computers, and in some instances, when accessing the internet from a public terminal, it cannot be done.

However, there are resources that are beginning to come to the aid of the beleaguered individual who wants everything in its place and a place for everything. It doesn't matter if that individual is a business person or a librarian, a start page can make life a lot easier, and using the internet a lot more effective. There are also specific uses that information professionals can make of start pages, and I'll look at those in some detail as well.

Let's start with start pages!

So, having taken a look at all of the problems, and having hinted at the way in which start pages can assist in all of these activities and overcome difficulties, what exactly are start pages? Quite simply, they are resources available on the internet, provided by third parties, that allow users to create their own home pages, with the content they choose, the look and feel they are comfortable with, available from anywhere. Obviously it does help that since the page(s) created are available at a specific URL users can set their browser defaults to go directly to their home page, pull it down off the net and display it on their own system. A change made directly to the home page will therefore be made when the user logs in via another machine. If a user is travelling and doesn't have access to their personal system they can still log onto their home page from an internet café, for example (while remembering in this instance not to make that the default home page for the browser on the machine that they happen to be using).

Start pages: disadvantages

So, a start page is a centralized resource, customized by each individual to reflect their own requirements, and held on a third-party website. The disadvantages of this approach need to be taken into account, of course. Unless you have a subscription to a resource with a commercial contract, you cannot rely on a start page. The company may go bust; it may decide not to develop the system; or it could close down the resource at any time it chooses. This is particularly the case with Web 2.0 companies which spring up overnight and disappear in a blink. If a user has not been sensible enough to keep copies of what they have created, with a separate list of all the links they have created and so on, it's going to be very hard to replicate it. It would be unwise to trust one's own memory here, since we can recall only a limited number of resources without assistance, and since the majority of start pages will have a lot of data on them it would be doubly foolish.

Another problem is that when a company first produces a start page it does so with every intention of getting an enthusiastic user community that is able to suggest improvements or additions to a service, and indeed is more than willing to write modules. The more popular a resource, the more modules are added, and the circle beneficially continues outwards. However, if the company is unable to gain that initial following, those individuals that started to use the system very early on will look enviously at friends who got involved with companies that were proving more popular. In other words, individual users are making a commitment of their time and resources, and if this is not reflected by others they will not get the functionality they wish unless they are capable of writing it themselves.

The provision of resources and functionality is not the same across the board, and one resource may be made available for one start page, but not for another. It is therefore very important to decide what aspects of a start page are necessities, which are desirable and which would be fun to have. Only once that initial shopping list has been created can the user choose which start page package is best for them.

Start pages: advantages

The list of disadvantages may look a little imposing, but, because there are so many advantages in using one of these resources, it really does make sense to explore the ways in which they can be used by an individual, a group or indeed an entire organization. Obviously each particular package will have certain elements that others do not, but there are certain things that they generally have in common.

You will be able to create a list of links to pages that you visit on a regular basis, much like a list of favourites or bookmarks displayed on the screen for you without any need to pull them down from a menu bar. You can also rename or label them if you need or want further personalization. While this will only save a few scant seconds, over time it will mount up the more that you use the start page, with all your top links immediately available.

Depending on the e-mail package you are using it may be possible to set up a start page module that will check your e-mail for you on a regular basis and display the title(s) of any unread messages that you have. Once again, this can save you time and effort and will mean that you only need to visit your e-mail account when you know for certain that you have mail waiting for you.

Most of us use search engines on a regular basis and designers of start-page utilities are aware of this, and have produced modules that allow a small search box to be located on a page, allowing users to run searches directly, instead of having to visit the search engine first.

Given the level of interest in RSS feeds it will come as no surprise to learn that feeds can also be put onto start pages, constantly bringing new data to the attention of the user. This might be news items from major news providers, favourite forums, weblogs, Google groups and so on – in fact anything that has an RSS feed can be included on a start page.

Most start-page resources provide a whole host of other modules that can be dragged and dropped onto a start page as needed. Obvious examples are links to Flickr accounts or groups, weather reports, small games, clocks, to-do lists, upcoming events, television schedules, chat options and so on.

A start page also allows users to create their page as they wish to, with modules in specific places, one, two or three columns, different colours, fonts and sizes, and so on. This is obviously important, since it's the page that users spend longest looking at, so it has to meet their personal tastes and feel comfortable to them.

A start page may well actually be rather more than one single page, and in many instances this will be vital – the more modules a user wants, the more complicated the page becomes. Logically therefore it makes sense to split up the content over several pages or tabs covering things such as work, home, fun, search and so on.

Finally, one last powerful feature of a start page is that it doesn't have to be limited to a single individual. Most are, of course, but there's no reason why this needs to be the case. Very few resources do yet allow this but some do, and this may well affect your choice. Such a resource allows the user to create a start page, or indeed an entire site, that can be used by a group of individuals in a library setting, for example.

Start pages in operation
Pageflakes

Pageflakes at **www.pageflakes.com** is a good example of a start-page resource. This was the winner of the SEOmoz Web 2.0 award for start pages in 2006 (details at **www.seomoz.org/web2.0**), beating opposition such as Netvibes (**www.netvibes.com**), Google's own personalization offering at **http://google.com/ig** and the Microsoft Windows Live resource at **http://live.com**. Pageflakes was acclaimed for its simplicity, clean style and the large number of 'flakes' or modules available to users.

Pageflakes is easy to use, and registration is straightforward. The initial page (shown in Figure 5.1 overleaf) is rather sparse, but it contains everything necessary to start using the system.

Users can choose items from the main 'flake' (Welcome to Pageflakes!) to create their initial start page, and can then view the page itself, which will look something like that shown in Figure 5.2 (overleaf).

Modules can be expanded or contracted on the page as necessary, simply by clicking on the triangle to the left of each title. More flakes can be added by clicking on the 'Add Flake' option in the top left-hand corner, and RSS feeds can be added just as easily; Pageflakes offers a variety of suggestions, or users can add their own favourites. Individual pages can be created, retitled, shared or published, as shown in Figure 5.3 (page 75).

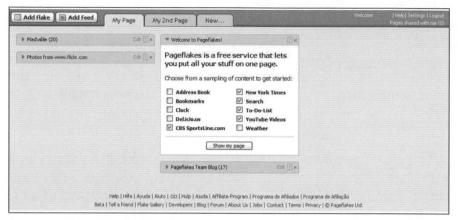

Figure 5.1 The initial Pageflakes interface

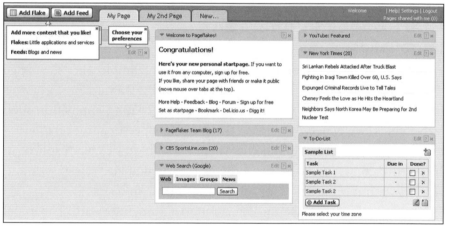

Figure 5.2 The Pageflakes start page

The ability to share or publish pages is one particularly powerful option that Pageflakes provides for its users. This means that individuals can share pages with their friends or with much wider audiences, depending on content. Consequently this turns a page into a proper community resource, and other users can create their own start page, but incorporate elements from other people as other tabs. Obviously the ability to write to, edit or otherwise amend someone else's page is strictly curtailed, but the 'shareability' aspect is the one to concentrate on. A 'finished' version of

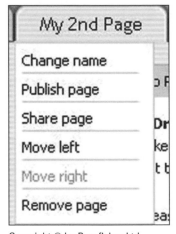

Figure 5.3
Individual Pageflakes page
options

the start page is shown in Figure 5.4, but of course the value of the system is that a start is never 'finished' – it should be constantly changing and evolving over time as the needs of the user change.

Other start-page utilities

As you would expect, Pageflakes is not the only resource available, and there are others that may be preferred in some instances. Another popular offering is Netvibes at **www.netvibes.com** which works in a very similar way to Pageflakes. The author's Netvibes start page is shown in Figure 5.5 (overleaf). Although it looks slightly different from that offered by Pageflakes, there is enough of a similarity to work out what the functionality of the different modules is. There are obviously differences – the web search functionality provides four different search engine tabs with the ability to have a default search sitting in the search box, for example, but each user will find pluses and minuses with each resource.

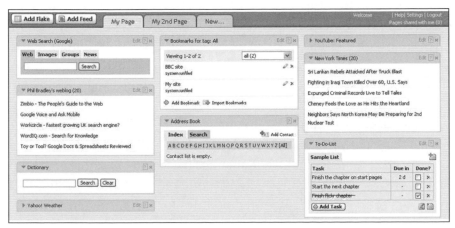

Figure 5.4 A 'finished' home or start page using Pageflakes

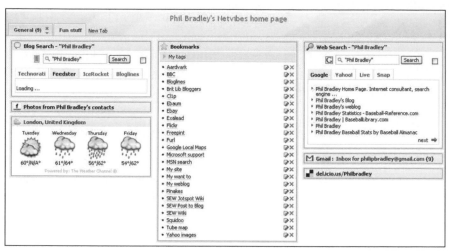

Figure 5.5 The author's Netvibes start page

Other utilities worth looking include Eskobo at **www.eskobo.com**, MyWebDesktop at **http://mywebdesktop.net**, Protopage at **http:// protopage.com/v2**, Start at **www.start.com**, Magnoto at **www.magnoto.com**, Favoor at **www.favoor.com** and Goowy at **www.goowy.com**.

Using start pages in a library setting

Unlike some of the other resources that we've looked at, start pages tend to be of much more use to the individual than to larger groups. Clearly they are easy to set up, change and edit as necessary, and importantly, because the data is stored on the systems of the provider of the resource, a personalized start page can be used on any computer that connects to the internet.

While start pages can be useful for everyone, and can be a great time saver, I think they have particular value for searchers and people who need to keep up to date with current affairs. The search-box modules mean that searches can be run quickly without the necessity of going to a particular search engine. Creating modules for various different search engines and then displaying them all on the same page is an effective way to remember that there are a lot of options available to searchers besides Google.

Embedded RSS feeds on a page are very helpful ways to keep on top of the constant flow of information across the busy professional's desk. Keeping a news reader or news aggregator open as a background tab or window is certainly useful, but even then it's necessary to flip back and view it on a regular basis. Having a few of the key RSS feeds there on the start page constantly keeps the professional up to date with what is going on in his or her world with absolutely no effort whatsoever.

As previously noted, the ability to share or publish start pages to a wider audience can also prove valuable. Of course, start pages can be created using straightforward HTML, and no one would deny that, but the advantage of a start page resource is that it can be done so much more quickly and effectively, with the addition of modules (such as weather forecasts) that cannot easily be put onto a 'home-made' page. Perhaps most importantly, the start page can be created by the most appropriate person – the librarian – without having recourse to, or the need to wait for, someone else such as a technician to build it. It's not even necessary to create a link to the start page from the organization's home page either – it's just a matter of changing the home page value in the browser. One issue obviously is that individual pages could be changed by malicious users, so this may be a solution only in very specific instances, but nonetheless it is worth considering. Within a small environment, or a library with only a small number of public access machines, it may be a superb way of providing access to a very wide variety of resources quickly and effectively, with minimal work on the part of the librarians.

Conclusion

Start pages are a perfect example of what Web 2.0 is all about – simple and straightforward in concept, highly adaptable to the needs of individuals and groups alike, and created without fuss or a need for detailed technical knowledge. Their ability to incorporate information from many other resources, such as websites and RSS feeds, and the production of specific modules to do particular tasks makes them an excellent resource that everyone can use on a regular basis. Irrespective of what software you use any start page resource will save time, effort and money – as well as making life much easier!

URLs mentioned in this chapter

www.eskobo.com

www.favoor.com

http://google.com/ig

www.goowy.com

http://live.com

www.magnoto.com

http://mywebdesktop.net

www.netvibes.com

www.pageflakes.com

http://protopage.com/v2

www.seomoz.org/web2.0

www.start.com

Chapter 6

Social bookmarking services

Introduction

One of the advantages of the internet is that you can always find something, somewhere related to your query or interest. Very often you know you will want to refer back to a specific page at some point in the future, so it's necessary to keep details of exactly where that page happens to be located. However, it's inadvisable to attempt to remember more than a few URLs, and even then they need to be short or memorable. Bookmarking pages, or listing them as Favorites, is obviously one solution, but there are more powerful alternatives. This chapter looks in detail at some of the other, more effective ways in which bookmarks and favourite pages can be stored for later retrieval. At first glance this would appear to be a very personal, very solitary activity, but as we'll see it is in fact quite the opposite of that, and a resourceful information professional can quickly and easily create a powerful collection that can be used by a much wider audience. On a brief terminological point, I am using the terms 'Bookmarks' and 'Favorites' as synonyms, since the main difference between them depends on which browser is being used.

Why bookmarks aren't enough

All browsers will provide some basic functionality for their users when it comes to bookmarking, and it's very easy to add page after page with very little thought – until the time comes when it's necessary to locate a specific page. Unless users are quite formal and organized in their approach it's likely that the bookmarks will very quickly turn into a morass of pages which are not stored in anything other than vague chronological order, which may or may not exist any longer and the titles of which may make no sense at all.

As an embarrassing illustration, my bookmark collection used to look like what you can see in Figure 6.1. If you think it's a confusing mess, don't worry: you're not the only one.

Figure 6.1 The author's bookmark collection

Of course, it's not just that the bookmark system is poor, relying as it has to on focus, organization and a thoughtful approach to the ordering of information (all of which librarians are good at, of course, but strangely often not when it comes to their own collections of information), but there are intrinsic flaws to the system. The titles of each page saved are taken from the original title of the page itself (to be found in the top left-hand corner of the browser window), and these are often uninformative. A few that I found in my own collection were gems such as 'Welcome to our site', 'Our home page', 'index', or simply 'Untitled'. Even though I thought a page useful when I first visited, I'm hardly going to remember why exactly I bookmarked a page with such a title in three months' time, and it's necessary to go back and view the page again to refresh my memory, all of which takes time. Moreover, the bookmark is simply doing exactly that – noting a particular page. It may no longer be available or the content may have changed, and in any case I can't see the content without re-viewing the page to retrieve the information that I want. Irritatingly quite often I cannot recall exactly which bookmarked page in the vast collection is the one that I want, thus rendering the information to all intents and purposes lost.

Another problem with bookmarking in this fashion is that the function is machine dependent: that is to say, you can bookmark a page on one computer and that is the only place that it's bookmarked, and in order to retrieve the information that exact machine has to be used again. This is annoying enough if you are using a computer at work and another at home, but if you are using any one of a bank of public machines there is no point in bookmarking anything at all.

Fortunately, however, this traditional approach to bookmarking can safely be consigned to Web 1.0 since there is now a wide variety of other resources available that the enthusiastic bookmarker can use with much greater functionality.

New bookmarking resources – new functionality

There is a wide variety of different types of bookmarking services, all with their own particular advantages and disadvantages. However, there is some functionality that almost all of them share which is worth discussing before looking at individual examples. Social bookmarking systems are one of the easiest ways to begin to get a really good appreciation of the power of Web 2.0 resources as they are easy to use, simple to set up, and gain in value as more people use them. At a basic level users create free accounts and will usually add an icon or link to their browser bar. When they find a web page that is of interest to them they can simply click on the link to add it to their collection of bookmarks.

No real change at this point to the 'old fashioned' system, but users are not storing the bookmark information on the computer they happen to be using at that particular instance; instead the details are stored on the server of the third-party bookmarking service. Moreover, users have the option to add information to the bookmark, rather than just saving it. Commonly this will include being able to put the bookmark in a particular folder (or sometimes multiple folders), and to 'tag' the bookmark. A tag is simply the description given to the activity of cataloguing or classifying a particular bookmark. A web page about Singapore might be tagged as 'Singapore, Asia, city, tourist, tourism, far east, holiday, travel', for example; it's entirely up to the person bookmarking the page to choose how to describe it.

For those of us with a training in such matters the idea of a controlled vocabulary comes to mind, which may perhaps give a rather more focused and accurate approach, but equally tagging by individuals does provide a broad, rich and varied approach that may otherwise be lacking. Some resources also allow users to add their own comments or descriptions about the page they are bookmarking to make it even easier to find in the future. The bookmark can be retrieved at some later date by running a search on any of the tags the user thinks are appropriate.

Of course, that's how a system can be used on an individual basis, but we can also consider the 'social' aspect of bookmarking as well. If someone else decides to tag the same page about Singapore the system is able to recall that it has been bookmarked before and can show a list of tags that have been used to describe it, and these can be used by the newest bookmarker in whole or in part, and they can of course add their own. Consequently over a period of time a community of users will between them tag a large number of pages in a rudimentary classification scheme into a database. Other users can then search bookmarked pages to find ones that cover their subject area of interest, safe in the knowledge that those pages returned from the search are almost guaranteed to be on topic. It is also possible to create tables of popular pages and various 'top ten' resources, which can be a good way to keep an eye on what people are bookmarking at any particular time. While this is useful it can also have the unfortunate effect that once a page is deemed to be popular many more people will attempt to visit it, with the result that access slows up, and in some cases the site may actually crash purely from the weight of numbers.

Specific social bookmarking resources

It is worth noting that this is one of the most populated areas of Web 2.0 resources, and there are hundreds of different resources that provide users with the ability to save bookmarks in one form or another. I have no doubt that it would be possible to write an entire book just on these resources alone, so it's even more important to make the point that the resources mentioned below are merely a representative collection of utilities, and should not be regarded as a comprehensive listing.

Furl

Furl (**www.furl.net**) is a free service that allows users to file complete web pages or URLs, annotate them, put them into appropriate folders (that they create) and to store them for as long as they are needed – literally File URLs. Pages can be retrieved through the search interface provided, and searches can be limited to specific folders or search terms, or across the entire collection of 'Furled' pages. Each user is allocated a total of 5 Gb of personal archive space, which is enough for tens of thousands of pages.

One important distinction between Furl and some of the other social bookmarking services is that Furl will save an entire web page, rather than just the URL and a user-created annotation. Consequently, in order to retrieve a particular web page, all a user needs to do is to remember some unique words on that page, or from their own description or tags in order to retrieve it. Clearly this makes Furl a particularly valuable resource for searchers and others doing research into particular areas, since all the guesswork is taken out of retrieving exactly the right page – it's almost as though users are just printing off copies of pages that they find, storing them and then getting instant recall.

This does not, however, mean that Furl is breaking copyright on a grand scale. Each page Furled by a user is available to be viewed by that specific user only and no other. If other people see details of Furled pages (in the public areas of the resource) and they click on them, they are immediately redirected to that specific page on the originating site – they cannot view the archived version of a page. It could therefore be argued that far from being a threat to the originating resource Furl is actually bringing it to the attention of a larger group than would otherwise have seen it.

The social element of Furl can be seen in a number of different ways. A visit to the site will immediately present a list of the most popular pages that have been Furled on that particular day, as can be seen in Figure 6.2.

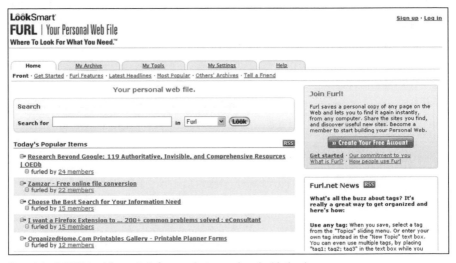

Figure 6.2 The Furl home page

This is interesting, of course, but is more in the nature of serendipity than anything else, although it could be argued that if there is a particular event or news item making the news it is likely that Furl users will have found helpful pages or resources and, as such, they will be a good starting point for any research into that particular subject area.

Rather more powerful is the ability that Furl has to recommend material to users, based on their specific interests. When someone registers with the service and begins to Furl pages that reflect their interests, the utility is able to match those pages to those Furled by other users and make the logical assumption that if users 1 and 2 have Furled pages A and B, user

3 who has furled page B will probably have an interest in page A as well. To give an example from my own experience, on the page of recommendations Furl offered me, of the first 25 items, 15 looked immediately interesting, with another five of passing interest to me.

Furl will also suggest 'Furlmates' to you, although the name implies a greater level of intimacy than is the case – it is simply a listing of people who share a reasonably high percentage of similar pages. It would be an error to simply dismiss this out of hand, since it is possible to subscribe to the lists created by other members – although you cannot view the actual pages Furled (as previously mentioned), you can see what they Furl using an RSS feed linked into your news aggregator. I have subscribed to the lists of a number of other users of Furl and often find some very useful nuggets of information that I would otherwise have completely missed.

The Furl system has a great many useful functions, and is easy to use. Figure 6.3 shows part of my own Furl archive: the screen shows a search that I am just about to run – a search on 'technological advances' in my 'Futurology' folder within the last three months. The links that are displayed below are those pages that have been recently added, with the

Figure 6.3 Part of the author's private Furl archive

page title to the left, date of addition to the archive, the topic or folder that pages have been assigned to, and the number of page views they have had.

Adding a page to a Furl collection is also very straightforward. Once the Furl link has been added to the browser it is simply a question of clicking on it when a user finds a page they wish to bookmark. This will bring up a dialogue box similar to that in Figure 6.4.

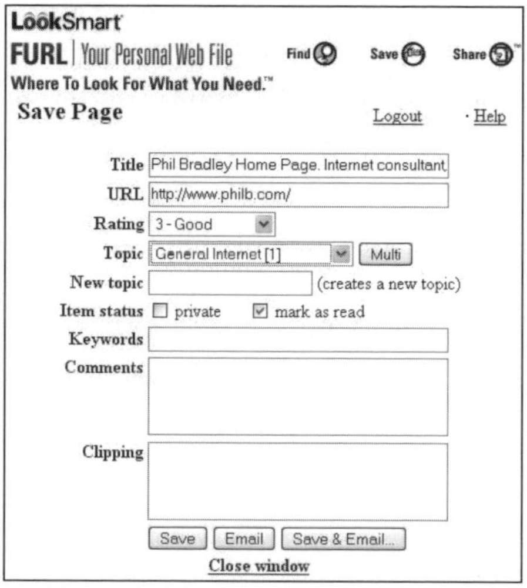

Copyright © 2007 LookSmart Ltd. Screenshot reproduced with thanks.

Figure 6.4 Saving a page with Furl

The title of the page can be edited if it doesn't make good sense, the page can be rated from 1 to 5, and it can be assigned to a single topic or multiple topics if appropriate. Alternatively a new topic can be created, and the item can be viewed as private (in which case it does not appear in a public profile) and is marked as read. Users may add further context to a page, and make it easier to remember, by adding in some keywords that they feel mirror the content of the page. They can also add any comments they feel are appropriate – that the saved page will be useful for a particular project, or a reminder to tell a colleague about the page. The clipping section allows a user to cut and paste a segment of the page they find useful, informative or which summarizes the content of page from the viewpoint of the original writer. The page itself and the added details can then be saved, and the details (without a copy of the original page) can also be e-mailed to friends or colleagues.

Sites added to a Furled collection can be publicized by using RSS for inclusion in a news aggregator, as a feed in something such as a start page, in a weblog or as a series of news items on a home page, for example.

Del.icio.us

If I were writing this chapter from a chronological perspective del.icio.us would have been the first social bookmarking service that I'd mention, since it was launched in September 2003. Del.icio.us is available at **http://del.icio.us** or the rather easier to remember **www.delicious.com**, but either will work perfectly well.

Del.icio.us is based on a slightly different concept from that of Furl, and is much more closely related to the concept of bookmarking from within the browser. Its primary purpose is to make your bookmarks available in one central store or repository that is available from any computer you want to use. Obviously you can bookmark anything that appeals to you – website pages, weblog articles, reviews, recipes. If you can put it into your own browser bookmarks, you can put it into your del.icio.us collection. Of course that is the bare minimum that you can do with the system; it has considerably more functionality than that. You can share your favourites with friends or colleagues, or indeed the whole del.icio.us community, which now numbers more than 1 million users (according to their weblog entry of 25 September 2006 at **http://blog.del.icio.us/ blog/2006/09/million.html**). Users can also use the system to explore new things that will be of interest to them.

Getting started with del.icio.us

Once you have signed up for an account with del.icio.us probably the easiest way to get started is to import your existing collection of bookmarks from your browser, and del.icio.us provides full instructions on this process. It also makes sense to install the del.icio.us browser buttons as well,

Figure 6.5 The del.icio.us buttons

since it makes the process of adding bookmarks that much easier, and they provide quick access to your collection. They can be seen to the right of the 'Home' icon in Figure 6.5.

Adding a new bookmark is simplicity itself – just clicking on the 'Tag' button brings up a dialogue box similar to that in Figure 6.6 (overleaf), and it's then just a job of filling in the description, notes and tags field to

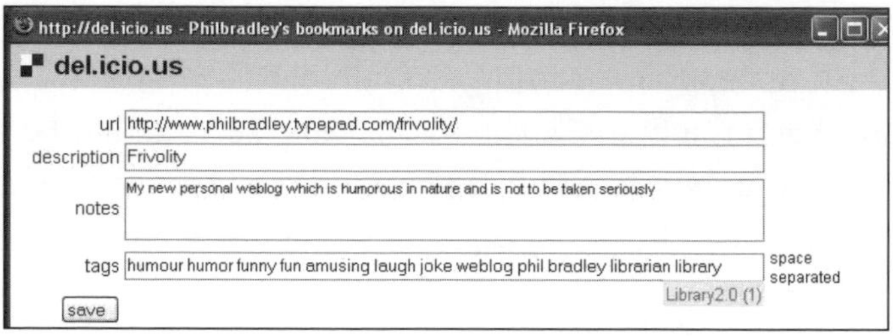

Reproduced with permission of Yahoo! Inc. © 2007 by Yahoo! Inc. YAHOO! and the YAHOO! logo are trademarks of Yahoo! Inc.

Figure 6.6 Adding a bookmark to a del.icio.us collection

accurately define the page that is being added. In fact, if the page has been previously bookmarked by other users del.icio.us will suggest tags for you, as can be seen in Figure 6.7.

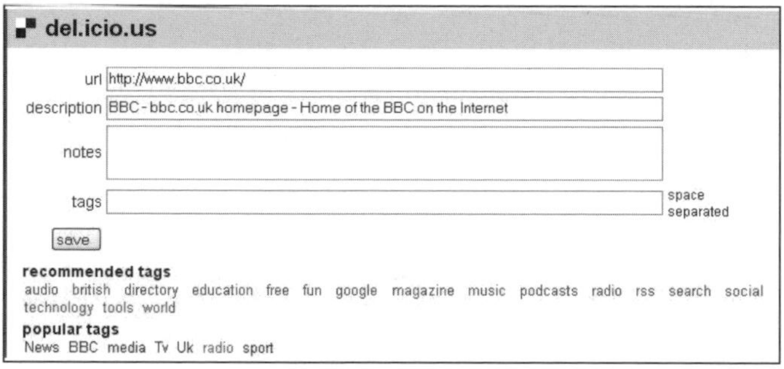

Reproduced with permission of Yahoo! Inc. © 2007 by Yahoo! Inc. YAHOO! and the YAHOO! logo are trademarks of Yahoo! Inc.

Figure 6.7 Tags for the BBC home page as suggested by del.icio.us

The ability to add tags to your bookmark collection obviously makes it much easier to find particular pages again in the future, without having to rely on memory, or the browser bookmarking folder system. It's possible to simply recall a set of bookmarks that use a particular tag and to further search within that. Del.icio.us will also display further information about a specific page, such as the number of other people who have added it to their own collections, and notes or comments that have been made about it.

The del.icio.us resource allows searchers to search for information using a search algorithm based on popularity, rather than search engine ranking. There are obviously flaws in this approach, because a large number of people simply bookmarking a page doesn't make it intrinsically good or useful – in fact it may have been bookmarked because it's particularly bad! However, a listing of popular sites based on del.icio.us bookmarking at **http://populicio.us/fulltotal.html** can be an interesting starting point for some research. Sites that have been added to the system recently are listed at **http://del.icio.us/recent** (this page gives an indication of the popularity of the service, as 24 sites had been added in the last minute when I looked), while popular pages are found at **http:// del.icio.us/popular**.

A very simple way to see which pages have been tagged with a specific word is to include it in the del.icio.us URL. For example, to see a listing of pages that have been tagged with 'CILIP' one simply needs to type into the browser address bar **http://del.icio.us/tag/cilip**, and this can be expanded to two or more terms by using the + symbol – so a search for sites that were tagged with both 'library' and 'innovation' would be **http://del.icio.us/tag/library+innovation**. Specific file types can be searched as well: del.icio.us does not limit users to text data, and it's possible to run a search for audio, video, image or document file types. A complete listing is posted at **http://blog.del.icio.us/blog/2005/06/casting_the_ net.html**. Finally, one can see the history of a web page and how it has been tagged by visiting the page http://del.icio.us/url and typing in a specific URL. Given that del.icio.us is a Web 2.0 based resource it should come as no surprise that all of these search strings, strategies and results can be saved as RSS feeds and incorporated into other sites and resources.

Using social bookmarking services in a library context

Clearly the ability to share bookmarks is invaluable on a personal basis, and overcomes the problems mentioned at the beginning of the chapter. That does not mean that there are not still problems with any of these systems – one of the largest being that not every computer you use will have the appropriate browser button(s) loaded, which does make the process slightly more complicated than it would otherwise be. Even if other computers do have the appropriate bookmarklet or link to a specific social bookmarking system, it doesn't necessarily follow that you would end up adding bookmarks to your own collection, since the bookmarklet may have been set up to add bookmarks to someone else's collection, and not to your own.

However, having said that, there are ways in which a social bookmarking service can provide a useful resource for its clients. Sensible use of RSS feeds is one of the most obvious ways of taking the data and presenting it in a different format. It is reasonably straightforward to create a web page, start/home page, portal or module for a weblog and then take a feed directly from resources such as Furl or del.icio.us. Given the ease of combining different tags, as with del.icio.us, all that an information service would need to do would be to create a tag for its own institution and tag everything the staff found with that (thus overcoming the problem of all using the same machine or account – each library staff member could have their own account as long as they all remembered to use the same institution tag) and then with other keywords as appropriate.

Depending on the users of the information centre and their particular information needs, it would also be possible to create further tags for particular projects that users were involved with. Any pages that provided useful information on the project could then be tagged and once again made available on an appropriate web page or other resource. Indeed, because of the social nature of the systems, feeds could be created by library staff tailored to exact requirements, and more general feeds without an institution tag to alert staff and users alike to the existence of other resources discovered by people who use that particular bookmarking service.

The information professional then begins to play the part of a filter for their users, by locating and highlighting the best material they can find. Of course, this does not stop users looking for their own material, but bookmarked collections of good-quality data will save them a considerable amount of time. It also provides another mechanism for staff to keep each other informed about new resources as they are discovered.

As well as using these resources to assist your own clients and inform them about the discoveries you are making and the resources you're publicizing, you should also be thinking of ways to use these services to keep yourself up to date with what's going on in the subject areas that interest you. It's always worth remembering that you are able to tap into as many of these services as you wish. Although you may decide to focus your own or your institution's efforts on one particular resource, there is no reason why you should not create RSS feeds from as many other resources as you wish. All the feeds can be kept in a news aggregator or on a start page and looked at periodically. If you discover an individual who appears to have the same type of interests, most resources will allow you to subscribe to the RSS feeds of the material they make publicly available. Social bookmarking services therefore allow you to identify experts or enthusiasts in particular subject areas.

A number of libraries are already using del.icio.us as a bookmarking system, such as San Mateo Library (**http://del.icio.us/SanMateoLibrary**), La Grange Park Library (**http://del.icio.us/LaGrangeParkLibrary**) and Lancing Public Library (**http://del.icio.us/lansingpubliclibrary**).

Other social bookmarking tools

As it is, relatively speaking, fairly straightforward to produce a social bookmarking system, this is an area that is heavily over-populated at the moment. The following is a listing of some of the other well known resources that are currently proving popular.

CiteULike

In an academic environment CiteULike at **www.citeulike.org** is very well known and respected. It's a free service that allows people (mainly academics) to share, organize and store the papers they are reading. The package automatically extracts all the citation details for the paper(s) and stores the data on the CitULike servers, allowing users access from any computer. Users can share their libraries, see what other people are reading and follow links from one paper to another, exploring new material that they would otherwise have been unaware of. The particular 'twist' of CiteULike is that users are able to export their collections into BibTeX or Endnote to create or add to a bibliography. If you are simply looking for a bookmarking service, however, CiteULike is probably not the best resource to use and the creator, Richard Cameron, in fact suggests del.icio.us in his written explanation of and background to CiteULike at **www.citeulike.org/faq/all.adp**.

Connotea

Another research oriented service is Connotea at **www.connotea.org**, run by the Nature Publishing Group, which was established in 2004 for researchers, clinicians and scientists. It has been specifically designed to work with resources such as PubMed and academic journals.

Diigo

A tool that has a rather broader approach, and which in fact could appear in various Web 2.0 categories, is Diigo, located at **www.diigo.com**. This combines social bookmarking with a clippings service, in situ annotation, tagging and sharing. Diigo lets users comment on web pages by using highlights and sticky notes that overlay the web page like a transparency (the nature of the web means it isn't of course possible for the notes to be added directly to a web page; they are simply made available via the Diigo system between one user and another). Diigo users can then read the comments left by others and add their own.

Further tools to check out

As previously mentioned, this is a very wide and quickly growing area. If none of the tools referred to has piqued your interest, here are a few others to try:

> BlinkList at **www.blinklist.com**
> Blogmarks at **www.blogmarks.net**
> BuddyMarks at **http://buddymarks.com**
> Ma.gnolia at **http://ma.gnolia.com**
> Netvouz at **www.netvouz.com**
> RawSugar at **www.rawsugar.com**
> Simpy at **www.simpy.com**
> Spurl at **www.spurl.net**
> StumbleUpon at **www.stumbleupon.com**
> Yahoo! My Web at **http://myweb.yahoo.com**

Choosing a social bookmarking service is worthy of a chapter in its own right, so before you make a final choice it's worth keeping a few things in mind.

Is the service you want to use mainly for yourself, or do you want to include other people in a combined effort? If the former, you can obviously choose whatever resource suits you best and just get on and use it. However, if you want others to use the same resource then it may well be worth checking with them first to see if any of the resources are already in common use.

Do you intend to publicize the bookmarks? If that's the case then you'll want to choose an option that will let you save the bookmarks in an RSS format to import onto a web page or similar resource.

Do you want to use social bookmarking as a research tool? It makes sense to learn only one application, so it's worth while spending some time exploring the search functionality to see if it will support the level and complexity of searching you may wish to do.

Do you simply need bookmarks, or is it important to have access to other functionality, such as sharing annotations, or saving full text? Not all bookmarking services can offer the entire range of functionality.

Do you want to import or export collections? An existing collection of bookmarks is a valuable resource, and it would be a shame to lose it. It may be appropriate to choose a service that will provide you with various options to save and manipulate your data.

Conclusion

In a very short space of time bookmarking has moved from a solitary activity based on the use of one computer to a global resource where individuals can share their interests, favourite resources and useful links with everyone. In order to fully utilize bookmarks it's always worth considering that if you think a resource should be added to your own list, it's highly likely that others will similarly find it helpful. Sensible use of tagging to identify individuals, organizations or both will create a powerful collection of links that can be widely used for a multiplicity of purposes.

URLs mentioned in this chapter

www.blinklist.com

http://blog.del.icio.us/blog/2005/06/casting_the_net.html

http://blog.del.icio.us/blog/2006/09/million.html

www.blogmarks.net

http://buddymarks.com

www.citeulike.org

www.citeulike.org/faq/all.adp

www.connotea.org

http://del.icio.us

http://del.icio.us/LaGrangeParkLibrary

http://del.icio.us/lansingpubliclibrary

http://del.icio.us/popular

http://del.icio.us/recent

http://del.icio.us/SanMateoLibrary

http://del.icio.us/tag/cilip

http://del.icio.us/url

www.delicious.com

www.diigo.com

www.furl.net

http://ma.gnolia.com

http://myweb.yahoo.com

www.netvouz.com

http://populicio.us/fulltotal.html

www.rawsugar.com

www.simpy.com

www.spurl.net

www.stumbleupon.com

Chapter 7

Build your own search engines

Introduction

In the early days of the internet we marvelled at the ability of search engines to find things for us. Just type in a few search terms, wait for a few moments and voilà – the search engine would return a series of results (often running into the millions if we'd done a poor search) matching our query to pages that would give us the answer to our question. Only of course it was never really quite so simple. Search engines have never been perfect at what they attempt to do, nor will they ever be; they can only do their best, but unfortunately that best is often not good enough.

There are a number of problems with search engines, of course, whether you are using Google, MSN, Yahoo! or any of the other hundreds that are available at the click of a mouse button. Most of them will provide the searcher with too much information, leaving them awash with too many daunting results. Even if a search is rather more focused (if the searcher is sophisticated enough to construct such a search, and this will naturally not always be the case), thousands of results may still appear. Most searchers will not look beyond the first page or so of results, and will simply hope to find something there to assist them in their query.

A second problem is that the search results cannot always be trusted. Search engines work on the basis that they cannot just return results to searchers in a random order – they need to be ranked in some sort of relevant order, and each of them employs a large number of algorithms to try to deliver the best and most accurate results possible. Unfortunately it is all too easy to confuse a search engine, and if the content on a web page is carefully constructed it can ensure that a less relevant page gets ranked more highly than a more helpful one. A general term for this is a 'googlebomb', and it can best be demonstrated rather than described. A simple search at the major search engines for the phrase 'miserable failure' in the past would often lead a searcher to the biography of George W. Bush. Leaving political opinion on one side, in most instances this result would not satisfy the enquirer. On a much more serious note, one of the sites returned by a search for 'Martin Luther King' purports to be a historical examination of the politician, but is in fact a poorly disguised racial attack, with little accurate or unbiased information available. There are many other examples, but I think that these suffice to illustrate that search engines have limits.

Searchers want better results from the search engines, and information professionals want to provide their users with the best possible information in the shortest amount of time. A good professional knows that simply to tell a user to find their answer in Google is not only a poor response to a question, but it may result in an incorrect response from the search engine to the original questioner. The way in which search engines work is coming under closer scrutiny and even the developers of search engines are attempting to change the way in which they provide information.

Consequently, the days when internet searchers had to accept what they were given from the search engines are disappearing. Search engines have been quick to pick up on the fact that users want to personalize the information they are getting – Google offers personalized searching, for example, and several other search engines allow a certain level of user intervention with search results. However, one development in particular has started to create a level of interest among searchers, and that is the ability to create your own search engine, and to search 'your way'. Well, not literally of course – unless you have millions of dollars available it's unlikely that you're going to start your own search engine from scratch, but if you have a few minutes to spare you can do the next best thing, which is to piggyback on the work of others and create a search resource that works the way that you want it to. Several resources are now available, and in this chapter I will take a look at some of the ways in which it is possible to almost literally create your own search engine. Specifically we have Rollyo (**www.rollyo.com**), PSS! (**www.pssdir.com**), the Yahoo! Search Builder (**http://builder.search.yahoo.com**), the Eurekster Swicki (**http://swicki.eurekster.com**) and the Google Custom Search Engine (**http://google.com/coop/cse**). Although they all claim to do the same job – create a search function for users – they all do it rather differently.

Rollyo

Rollyo, or 'Roll Your Own search engine', is probably the most familiar search-engine creator, since it's been around for some time. In common with the other resources it is a free utility – you just have to register to make use of it. Figure 7.1 shows the introductory Rollyo screen, which is simple and straightforward. It's important to choose a sensible name for the search engine (or, as Rollyo term it, 'searchroll') so that it's memorable and indicates clearly what the subject focus is – although given that you have only 20 characters available it's becoming increasingly difficult to manage

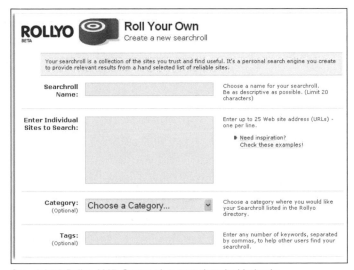

Copyright © Rollyo 2007. Screen-shot reproduced with thanks.

Figure 7.1 The Rollyo 'Create a new searchroll' screen

that successfully! Don't worry about getting everything absolutely perfect at this stage – you can always go back into the system at a later time and edit any and all the details as needed.

The process of creating a searchroll is very simple – just decide on the subject matter, and choose up to 25 websites that you feel are authoritative or representative, or just plain favourites that relate to the subject.

These sites are the ones that the searchroll will use when searching for information, and this is an important point to emphasize – with the Rollyo offering your main task is to include good-quality sites and exclude everything else. What the utility will do when a search is run is to search for 'Your term AND (site 1 OR site 2 OR site 3 .... OR site 25)'. Consequently it's very important to choose what you regard as the best sites, since the searchroll won't fall back on a more general search unless you explicitly tell it to. Rollyo is powered by Yahoo! and search results follow a specific order – sponsored results or links, custom news results and custom web results.

One of the strengths of Rollyo is that a lot of functionality has been added to a very simple concept, while (and this is the important point) keeping it simple. Once a searchroll has been created the owner can keep it private, or allow other people to use it, and they don't even have to have registered with Rollyo. One of my searchrolls is called 'Net searching' and is designed to be used by people who have an interest in search engine technology and developments. It's freely available at **http://rollyo.com/ philbradley/net_searching** and you can try it out for yourself. Alternatively, just take a peek at it in Figure 7.2.

It's possible to put a searchroll onto your own site or weblog, for example. Searchrolls can be incorporated onto websites by cutting and pasting the HTML that is provided and you're ready to go. Well, almost, because I found that the default presentation option was very small and fiddly, so I had to play around with the code for a few minutes to get something that I was happy with, but someone without any experience of HTML might struggle a little bit at this point. Figure 7.3 shows the result.

You can use the Rollyo bookmarklet to search your rolls, or the site that you're on without any fuss. Searchrolls can also be added to your Firefox search box, making it very easy to search for exactly the information you

Copyright © Rollyo 2007. Screen-shot reproduced with thanks.

Figure 7.2 Results screen from the author's 'Net searching' Rollyo searchroll

Copyright © Rollyo 2007. Screen-shot reproduced with thanks.

Figure 7.3
The 'Net searching' searchroll on a web page

need from a list of sites that you trust. Rollyo also enables users to create searchrolls by uploading their bookmarks, which can then be used as a starting point.

In summary, Rollyo is very good at a very simple task, and the addition of new utilities ensures that it's a very valuable resource. If you have a specific subject area that interests you, or you want to create something of a 'walled garden' for users to search in, I would definitely recommend taking a look at it in detail. It's simple, fast, effective and flexible.

PSS!

PSS!, or Personal Search Syndication, is a newcomer to the world of personalized search builders. Like the others mentioned here, it is free, although a premium service is being considered. Having registered, you create your PSS and an associated URL, hosted by PSS! (though, as with Rollyo, it can be included on your own website or weblog). The next stage is to configure the search itself. It was at this point that I was slightly disappointed with the service: I was limited to a total of 24 terms in six rows of four, and these were put together with an AND operator. So I could create a search for 'search AND engine AND technologies AND developments', but not 'search AND engine AND technologies AND developments AND innovations'. Alternatively I could include in the PSS 'search AND engine' OR 'search AND engines'. I was given no opportunity for phrase searching or anything that even vaguely resembled a complex search. It's fair to say that I could also include four terms to exclude from the search, but again, this is not impressive. The configuration screen was very bare, with limited help facilities, and only when I'd actually done the configuration of the search and seen what happened as a result did I really appreciate what I was supposed to be doing. Figure 7.4 shows part of the process of building the search

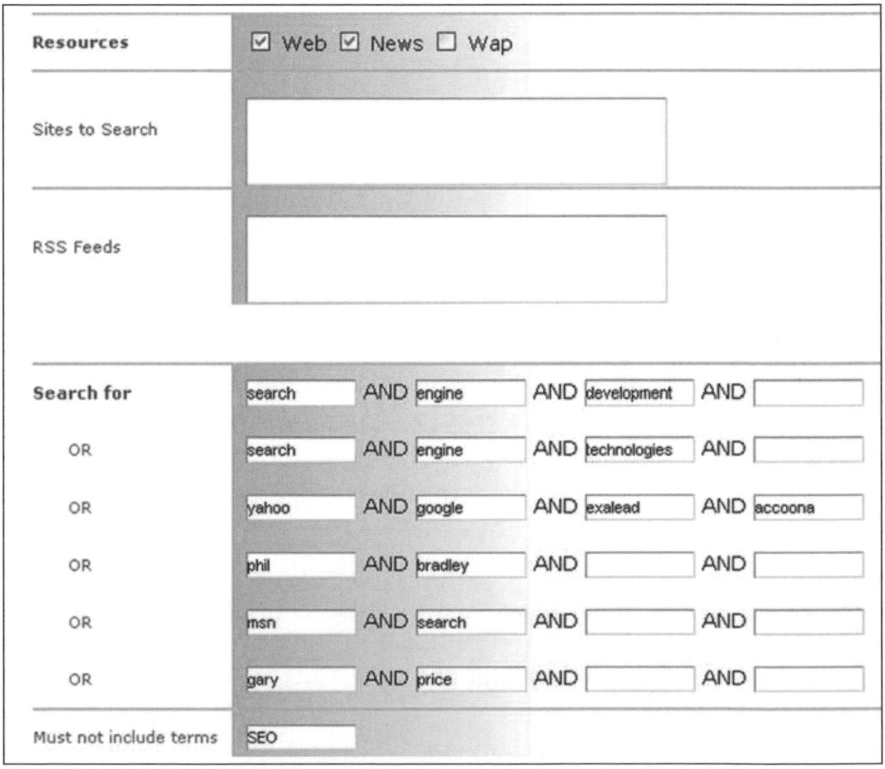

Resources	☑ Web ☑ News ☐ Wap			
Sites to Search				
RSS Feeds				
Search for	search	AND engine	AND development	AND
OR	search	AND engine	AND technologies	AND
OR	yahoo	AND google	AND exalead	AND accoona
OR	phil	AND bradley	AND	AND
OR	msn	AND search	AND	AND
OR	gary	AND price	AND	AND
Must not include terms	SEO			

Figure 7.4 Building a search with PSS!

Once the PSS has been created for you it takes about half an hour before you can see any results, and then these are updated for you on a daily basis, with the addition that you can create specific search alerts that are e-mailed to you, and there is also the nice option of getting the data via RSS. Results (and I don't know how the results are obtained in any detail, other than 'Our automated search agents crank away in the background to find relevant content on the Web that matches your described subject matter') are displayed in relevance-ranked order or by 'date insertion'.

The results themselves did not inspire me with a great deal of confidence. Having primed my PSS with terms related to search engines the no. 1 result when arranged chronologically was a website related to boxing and aerobics, without any mention of search engines at all. The first article that I felt related to my search was actually no. 5, and to be fair the next five results were also on topic. Admittedly I could then go back and delete inappropriate sites, or individual results, but this is very time-consuming, and would be unnecessary if it were possible to create sensible complex searches in the first place.

I can see that PSS! could be useful if you need to keep up to date with a particular subject area, and can define the nature of your enquiry with some very basic keywords or search syntax. However, I did not feel that PSS! would adequately replace my canned MSN searches or Google News Alerts. To be fair, that is only part of what the PSS! team wants to achieve, and the emphasis is on syndicating a personal search, so it may well be a useful addition to a librarian's armoury if they need to run a lot of updating searches for a large number of clients. More development work with the ability to create more complex search strings could, however, pay dividends, so I'll continue to keep an eye on it.

Yahoo! Search Builder

Yahoo! has recently turned towards personalized search builders with its Yahoo! Search Builder offering. The process of creating the search was very similar to the other offerings – naming my search being the first requirement. I then had to decide on which resources were to be searched, and was presented with three options – the web, a specific site or Yahoo! news, or any combination thereof. It was also possible to further customize the experience for my users – a custom search based on sites that I trusted (along the Rollyo lines), keywords appropriate to the search, and the exclusion of certain keywords or sites.

The first section was easy to do: list five major sites. The second section, choosing keywords, was rather more difficult, and this is a problem that I have with all of these home-grown search engines. Obviously I could put in terms such as 'search', 'searching', 'search engines' and so on, but by the very nature of the sites that I was choosing to include that was going to be a given. Moreover, by adding terms, I presumed that this would simply create an AND function, so a lot of synonyms wouldn't actually help the searcher, and indeed might well hinder them. 'Information' seemed to be a sensible term to use, however, so I went with that. Similarly with the next section I chose terms to exclude from the search. This was in some ways easier, since I could choose a whole bunch of inappropriate terms; I wouldn't have thought anyone would be that interested in penguins when doing a search about search engines, but is there any point in excluding a term like that anyway? However, since I wasn't really interested in the stocks-and-shares aspect of search engines, there were a couple of related terms to exclude from the results. Finally I could exclude results from various sites (again, I have no idea how many) so I played it safe by excluding Disney). Ironically I couldn't restrict the search *to* specific sites – the earlier option just allowed me to choose several sites to emphasize. This is apparently something that is currently being addressed by Yahoo!, and from the searches I've been running it appears to be fixed; all of the searches that I ran were limited to the sites that I specified.

Of course at this point I did wonder if these choices were going to be public; it would be very easy to create a search engine that excluded the results from my major competitor, for example, thus creating a nice bias in favour of my own site. The system was not helpful on this point, so I'll just have to wait and see. 'Search preview' seemed to do what it's supposed to do, and I was happy with the results at this point.

I could also customize on the news front by time period (I was going for the last day's worth of news) and this time I wasn't limiting by site – I wanted any news I could find. There was also an option to include or exclude from different categories, such as politics and entertainment, but again I went for all options.

My options here having been chosen, the next page allowed me to customize by size (narrow, wide or customized). I could also show most popular searches, change the colours and fonts used, and choose the site encoding. I chose default options for all of these.

The next page allowed me to customize a little further, with some banner text ('Phil Bradley helps you search more easily') which is required, oddly enough. I could also include a logo if desired, with colours and fonts. Finally I was able to choose to open results in a new window, and limit to a particular language, and I could cut and paste the resulting code onto a web page for the world to use. The search box was clear, with three options – search the web, this site or news. When I ran my search I was then taken directly to the Yahoo! site and my results were displayed in the usual format, together with a note that the results had been customized for me. Figure 7.5 shows the search box as it appeared on my own page, and Figure 7.6 shows the results page once a search had been run.

Reproduced with permission of Yahoo! Inc. © 2007 by Yahoo! Inc. YAHOO! and the YAHOO! logo are trademarks of Yahoo! Inc.

Figure 7.5
The Yahoo! search box

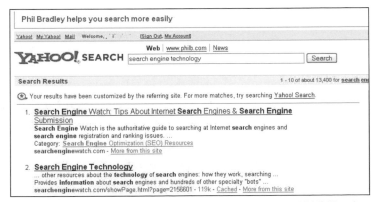

Reproduced with permission of Yahoo! Inc. © 2007 by Yahoo! Inc. YAHOO! and the YAHOO! logo are trademarks of Yahoo! Inc.

Figure 7.6 The results of search using the Yahoo! Search builder

Yahoo! Search Builder does exactly what it promises. It quickly creates a usable, functional search resource that focuses on the needs of the particular user. Given that it's a Yahoo! product I can see that this will become a popular feature very quickly and will be appearing on a lot of sites in the not-too-distant future.

The Eurekster Swicki

The next resource that I want to include here is the Eurekster Swicki. A swicki is the generic name that Eurekster has given to its user-built search engines. I'll explain in detail below exactly what this means but, if you're really in a hurry, it's a search engine that learns from, and has its results changed by, its user community. The Eurekster Swicki has again been available for some time and is a well known product. The emphasis here, however, is slightly different – instead of being based solely on an individual its strength is in its community appeal. If a group of people with a common interest can collaborate to create and then use a swicki, the results will quickly become tailored for that group.

Creation is straightforward. The swicki has to be named (and a nice piece of functionality here shows whether the name being typed is available or not), and the physical look of the search box is chosen from seven different options. You can then choose words or phrases to 'seed' the hot-searches cloud, together with options such as font and font size, and add keyword options and specific sites, blogs and maps to search. You can exclude specific sites and allow or disallow adult sites. After naming and categorizing the swicki the final step is simply to cut and paste the HTML code onto a web page or into a weblog, and also allow friends or colleagues to use it as well. The more people that use the swicki, the better it can 'learn' what results are appropriate for a search, and it can fine-tune the results, giving the entire community a better search experience. The swicki I use on my own website is shown in Figure 7.7, with the results shown in Figure 7.8.

Figure 7.7
The Eurekster Swicki search box on the author's site

Towards the end of 2006, Eurekster added new

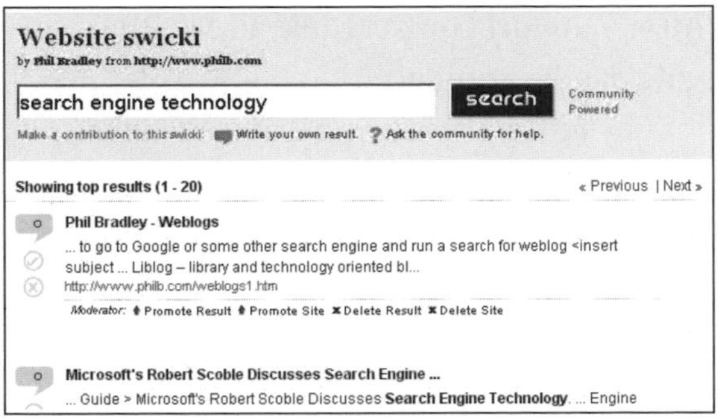

Figure 7.8 The results of a search run using
the Eurekster Swicki

functionality to further leverage the use of a swicki by its community.
Results can be 'voted' for and raised higher in the list of results, or
alternatively deleted. Users can also write their own comments that are
seen by other swicki users, and there is also a function available for users
to ask the community for help if they are having problems with a query.
All of this is moderated by the owner of the swicki, who retains complete
control over the resource.

Google Custom Search Engine

Google has been rather late to get into this particular area, and is the most
recent entrant of those considered here. However, if for no other reason
that its name, it will have to be taken seriously. Search creators can
choose to limit searches to specific sites, or simply emphasize specific sites
to more closely match and tailor the results to the interests of their user
groups. There is no limit to the number of sites that can be used; unlike
Rollyo, users may choose to develop a search engine that searches several
thousand sites, for example.

There are a few other differences between this option and the others
that have been discussed. Google offers users their own home page to host
the search box and various 'gadgets' to allow users to add sites to the
custom search engine(s) they have created. I created one that searches
librarian weblogs, for example: it is available at **http://google.com/
coop/cse?cx=004398262872497826460%3Aghzabap0tjo** or the rather

more sensible **http://tinyurl.com/ycrqek**, and it can be seen in Figure 7.9. The search engine can be configured to allow other people to volunteer to contribute to it by adding more content for example, and advertising can either be allowed or disabled, if the search engine is to be used primarily within a non-profit, academic or government site. Figure 7.10 shows the way in which new pages or sites can easily be incorporated into an existing search engine, which allows it to grow and develop over time using the Google Marker bookmarklet.

Screen-shot reproduced with thanks.

Figure 7.9 The Librarian Weblogs custom search engine provided by Google

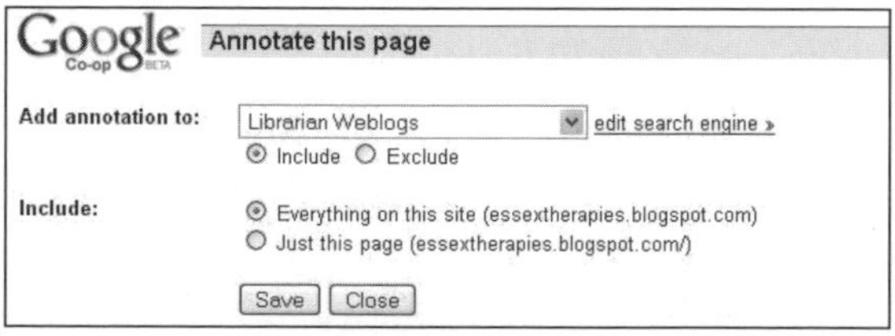

Screen-shot reproduced with thanks.

Figure 7.10 Adding a site to a custom search engine using the Google Marker

Library use of search engine builders

I can see a lot of ways in which a library might want to use these resources, or indeed a number of them. They are particularly useful in circumstances where:

- end-users tend to be naive and unsophisticated searchers
- there are a great many sites that provide similar information
- specific searches may (because of content or terminology) lead to inappropriate or misleading results
- searches lead to a lot of results
- users need guidance or assistance in choosing the most appropriate sites to use.

A page on an information department website could list a great many search boxes, and additional content could be used to guide the users towards specific ones depending on the type of query they have. Moreover, because the search boxes are easy to adapt and edit, the information professional can always ensure that the users are receiving data from the most reliable sources quickly and effectively. There is no reason why your own website should not be included in any or all of the searches that are created: it's a good way of really being sure about the results that users are obtaining!

All of these resources have different advantages and disadvantages, and it would be invidious to say that any one of them is the best or worst, since they're all doing slightly different things, albeit in the same general area. None of them stands head and shoulders above the others, but if for no other reason than the companies behind them, I would have to say that both the Yahoo! Search Builder and Google Custom Search Engine are going to dominate the market reasonably quickly. Nevertheless, choice is going to be very much down to individual requirement, and I confidently predict that while there are few utilities currently in this area it is going to get very busy very quickly.

Conclusion

One of the 'holy grails' of internet searching has always been the desire to make the results from any search more accurate, but of course what is accurate to one searcher is completely incorrect for another. While search engines are constantly striving to provide better results and are changing their ranking systems on a regular basis, the most that they will ever be able to offer is an off-the-peg service. However, with the addition of search builders, produced either by the major search engines themselves or by their smaller competitors, the searchers are now – for the first time, really – in a position to take over some control of the system and to decide for themselves just what an accurate search actually is. This is an area that is only going to grow in the coming years, as the concepts of search, personalization, and local search based on where you happen to be becomes the norm. The search builders mentioned in this chapter are not there yet, but they are useful and are pointing us in the right direction.

URLs included in this chapter

http://builder.search.yahoo.com

http://google.com/coop/cse

http://google.com/coop/cse?cx=004398262872497826460%3Aghzabap
    0tjo

http://rollyo.com/philbradley/net_searching

www.pssdir.com

www.rollyo.com

http://swicki.eurekster.com

http://tinyurl.com/ycrqek

Chapter 8

Creating and using websites and pages

Introduction

If you're slightly puzzled by the chapter heading, I don't blame you. After all, web pages and websites have been around for a long time, and despite innovations in HTML code, frames, Flash, JavaScript and so on they're not that different from what they were like a decade ago. However, there are major differences between the more 'traditional' web pages and sites and those available within a Web 2.0 environment.

With traditional pages if you wished to make a change to the content it was quite a long-drawn-out process. First of all you needed to have an understanding of how HTML worked, which either required hours of study or a course to get you up to speed. Then you would have to start your authoring tool – FrontPage or Dreamweaver or whatever – and make the change to your content. Prior to uploading this a good author would check their content to make sure it worked correctly, then upload it onto the server using FTP. Even then the process wasn't over, since diligence would dictate checking the page once more to make sure that everything worked the way it should do, and starting the whole process from scratch if it didn't. Of course, that's how it worked if you knew what you were doing. If you didn't, you would need to brief a technical colleague who could undertake the task for you. Content management systems (CMSs) (software packages that simplify the creation of web pages or sites, and which are generally used across an entire organization to ensure that content and pages all conform to one standard) have made the process a little bit easier, it's fair to say, but with that simplicity comes a more rigid structure and approach. However, whichever method was employed it could be a painful and prolonged experience leading to tears before bedtime.

Within a Web 2.0 environment things have changed radically. Websites can be created quickly and easily without any knowledge or understanding of HTML pages can be put together with drag and drop modules; complex functionality is no longer the exclusive province of the technical programmers; and updating can be done within seconds. This chapter looks at some of the things that can be achieved with various tools, and at some of the ways in which this simple creative approach changes the way in which information can be made available and, more importantly, shared.

Creating a resource page

The new resources now being made available allow users to create pages very quickly, and to integrate them with a variety of other utilities. Consequently one of the ways in which a page may be used is to quickly pull together a variety of resources on a specific subject area and perhaps across a number of different media to answer a specific need. A good example of a resource that does this is Squidoo, available at **www.squidoo.com**.

Squidoo works on the theory that people who are expert in a particular subject area, or who have a particular passion or interest in a subject, are in the best position to tell other people about that subject by providing access to good, trustworthy, high-quality resources. They become, in effect, creators of small niche-based directories, publishing data. Users build what are referred to as 'lenses': single-page subject-specific collections. These can be used for a variety of reasons – obviously to share knowledge, to bring groups of people together, to increase your own or your organization's profile, to increase the traffic to your own site or to earn money – though it should be pointed out that this last reason is seldom high on anyone's list, since you will not become a millionaire overnight.

Creating a lens

Once registered with Squidoo you can move on to create a lens. Give it a title, decide what you want to do with it from the available options – which will most likely be to get information out to people – and choose a URL, topic and some keywords from the step-by-step guide. This will create the lens for you, and then it's time to move onto the interesting bit, which is of course adding the content. The lens that I created for this chapter is at **www.squidoo.com/web2inyourlibrary**. You can see the screen used to edit the lens in Figure 8.1. This lens, while not having any 'real' content, does provide some ideas and hints on creating a lens, so rather than consider it as an example just hidden in the book, do feel free to visit it.

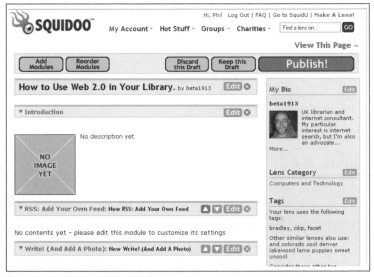

Figure 8.1 A Squidoo lens in the making

Your screen will obviously look slightly different, but the layout should be recognizable. You may wish to jump straight in and start to add content, in which case click on an 'Edit' button on one of the modules and put some material onto your page. Alternatively you might want to spend a little longer exploring some of the different modules available for use with a lens. Simply scroll to the bottom of the page and click on 'Add modules'.

Different modules for different purposes

Squidoo provides its users (or Lens Masters) with many different modules to let them customize their content. Probably the most important one is the 'Write' module, and you can use this to add whatever content you choose, and add a photograph as well. Figure 8.2 shows this module being edited.

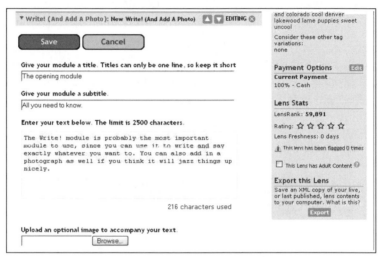

Figure 8.2 Editing a Squidoo module

There are, of course, other modules that are particularly useful for information professionals wishing to create content for their users. The RSS feed allows you to add data from a feed, or collection of feeds if you prefer. This could include a feed from your own weblog if you want to feed traffic back to that, or news headlines, or a set of search results. Add the URL, decide how many headlines you wish to show, decide if an excerpt should be included and how often it should be updated, and you're done. If you want to add another feed, either create another module or consider using one of the resources mentioned in Chapter 2 that will create a single feed based on several others.

You can encourage more awareness of what you or your colleagues are doing by adding a del.icio.us link (**http://del.icio.us**). This could either be to your own collection, which you can create by using your user name, or by tag.

Images culled from Flickr may also be a useful option, depending of course on the content of the lens, but even something as unphotogenic as Web 2.0 in a library setting produces some pictures that can be included. Before adding this module it's sensible to visit Flickr at **www.flickr.com** and do a quick search just to make sure there are some good images, though, and you'll also need the URL of each image, since they have to be added individually. It's worth mentioning that you don't need to be a member of Flickr, or to have any photographs there yourself, in order to use this module.

A reading list can be created quickly and easily by using the Amazon option. Either choose specific titles for your reading list, or provide some tags, and Amazon will choose titles automatically – while this choice looks like the easiest option at first, you will probably need to fine-tune the tags used.

There are many other options available to users, but it would be tedious to go through each of them individually, and many of them will not be applicable for the content you're thinking of concentrating on. However, it's worth just briefly mentioning a few more to whet your appetite. Google Maps (**http://maps.google.com**) will allow you to add a map to let people know where you are based, or to highlight a specific place, and a guestbook option allows people to communicate with you, to share information back and forth, and to create a real community feeling about the page. News headlines are available from the BBC or CNN, and 'Make a list' is a module that lets you create a bullet-point list, which can be really helpful if you are using a module as a teaching aid, or you wish to ensure that readers do actually read the content, rather than skip past it. There is a 'Polling' option that could be useful to engage with your audience: simply ask the question, choose the possible answers and see what the readers think.

Editing the finished page

Once you have decided on the modules you wish to use in the lens, they can quickly and easily be reordered on the page into the correct position. When you are happy that the lens does what you want it to, you can publish it for the world to see. Of course, you can then go back and re-edit it on the page, so in that sense it's inaccurate to say that the lens is 'finished', because a good lens will always be adapting to changes. Figure 8.3 shows the lens once the basics have been added.

Copyright © Squidoo LLC 2007. Screen-shot reproduced with thanks.

Figure 8.3 The Squidoo lens with some of the basics now in place

When the lens is published people obviously need to be made aware of it, so it's worth e-mailing contacts to inform them that you've got a lens up and running. You can also mention it in your weblog or on your own site, or find another Squidoo group that's concentrating on the same area as your own lens and make connections from within the wider Squidoo community.

However, that's not the end of the options with this particular resource: there are other things that can be done to further utilize the functionality of a Web 2.0 resource. You may have noticed that there are adverts on the page, as provided by Google. This is how the owners of the resource make their money: every time someone clicks on an advert, the owner of the website that 'owns' that advert pays Google a sum of money, and part of that is passed on to Squidoo. A proportion of that money can also be passed on to the owner of the specific lens, but owners can choose to donate all or part of that money to a charity.

It's very easy to keep an eye on the lenses you have created. As I'm sure you're expecting by now, each lens has an RSS feed, so you can simply add that to your new aggregator, and when anything changes – someone adds a comment, for example – you'll be informed straightaway.

If you wish to add something to a lens, the process is very simple and straightforward, and in many cases it's not even necessary to visit the lens itself. Squidoo provides lens authors with a bookmarklet that sits in the browser window. Consequently, if you are browsing the internet and find a resource you think would be a useful addition to the page you can click on the bookmarklet and add that resource to the appropriate lens (if you have more than one) and to the specific section of the lens. Figure 8.4 illustrates the dialogue box in which I am currently being prompted to add Facet Publishing to the lens previously created in this chapter.

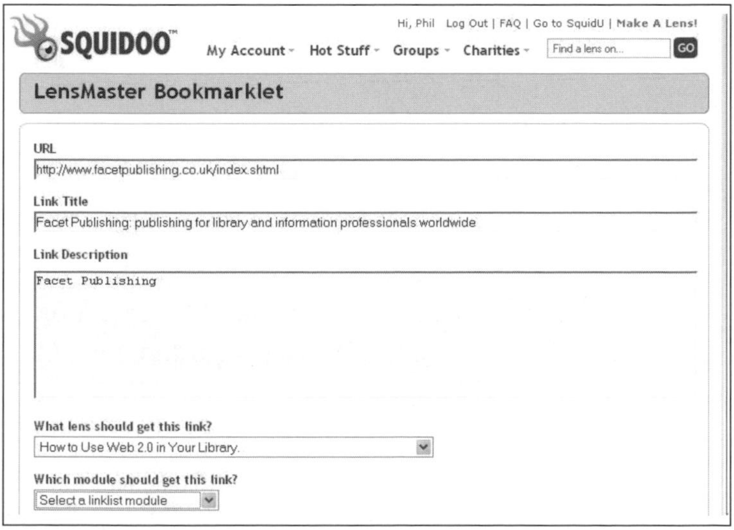

Figure 8.4 Adding a web page to an existing Squidoo lens

Using Squidoo within a library setting

A large number of libraries are already making use of Squidoo in a variety of different ways; a search just on 'library' returned over 300 results, and 'library web 2' gave me over a dozen different lenses. Some interesting examples of the options available to information professionals are:

- *creating a lens to focus on a particular area or region*
  the State Library of Pennsylvania has a lens for 'researching all things Pennsylvania' at **www.squidoo.com/State_Library_of_ Pennsylvania**
- *using lenses for training purposes*
  Michael Stephens has produced a lens as background for a course he runs at his university, at **www.squidoo.com/LIS701Dom**
- *using lenses to make a reading list, or form part of a presentation*
  Michael Stephens and Jenny Levine created a lens for people interested in the concept of Library 2.0 at **www.squidoo.com/ library20**
- *providing some humorous content – break out of the stuffy librarianship stereotype!*
  Stupid Library Tricks at **www.squidoo.com/librarytricks** is a collection of videos, links, a poll and products to buy, all of which look at the fun side of being in a library
- *discussion lenses*
  OPAC comparisons and library sites at **www.squidoo.com/opac** offer thoughts, ideas and topics related to online public access catalogues
- *short guides*
  a short useful guide to LISA (Library and Information Science Abstracts) is available in the lens at **www.squidoo.com/LISAHELP**
- *new books*
  either books added to the information centre, or just newly published work in a particular area, such as Science Technology and Management in the example at **www.squidoo.com/ monitorlinks**
- *using a lens to promote a library service*
  a nice example from Exeter Public Library in Rhode Island is at **www.squidoo.com/exeterpubliclibrary**.

Clearly therefore there are a variety of ways in which Squidoo lenses can allow librarians and other information professionals to quickly create resources that supplement existing work, or provide a mechanism to establish a web page that concentrates on a specific subject area. A lens can form the basis for an ongoing resource, or simply be used as a stopgap to quickly produce some material for a course or presentation, and the lens can either be left as an archival record, or deleted as appropriate. Squidoo, however, has its limitations (it is not possible to add different pages to a Squidoo lens, for example), so before embarking on a voyage of discovery it may be worth considering what other options are available.

Using portal-based services

Squidoo is based very much on the idea of the individual talking to a group in a 'lecture' style, by choosing the resources and keeping complete control of them. Of course there's nothing wrong with that in principle, and as a communication style it has a lot of advantages. However, it is only one style, and it's equally important to recognize that other approaches offer different benefits. For example, one Web 2.0 tenet is the concept of the 'wisdom of the crowd'. It is perfectly reasonable to assume that a group or community has a large amount to contribute to a subject or discussion, and this is where it makes sense to look at ways in which an entire community can start to get involved, and how an information professional can create a resource that not only allows but encourages such an approach. One answer to this (but of course by no means the only one) is a resource called Zimbio, at **www.zimbio.com**, which styles itself as 'The people's guide to the web'. Zimbio has created a set of tools and offers space for groups of people to work together to create public portals that focus on a subject in order to quickly gain an understanding of it. While in many respects this is similar to Squidoo the emphasis, as we shall see, is on community involvement to a far greater degree.

Establishing a community portal with Zimbio

As with Squidoo, the process of creating a resource is reasonably straightforward, and made all the simpler with some forethought as to exactly what the purpose of the resource is. It's a five-stage process to physically set a portal up and running, but it's quite possible to do one in no more than a few minutes. The first step is to give the portal a name, assign it to a category, make it public or private create a brief description, and add some keywords.

You are then prompted to add some useful links, so it is as well to have some of these already prepared and available. Step 3 is to set up a news tracker, with the option of using one of four different search engines, and step 4 provides you with the opportunity of doing the same thing again, but this time for images. The final stage is to inform friends and colleagues that the portal has been established, but given that it's almost completely empty at this point this might be a step that is worth skipping.

Once you have gone through that process you will then automatically be taken to the home page of the portal, which will look something like that seen in Figure 8.5. At this point you have a variety of different options available. You can add content to the page; edit the layout; e-mail the page to other people; add more links; post a topic to the forum; add, edit or delete the keywords used in the blog search or news-tracker services; or even add a photograph of yourself.

Copyright © 2007 Zimbio, Inc. Screen-shot reproduced with thanks.

Figure 8.5 The Zimbio guide associated with this book

Figure 8.6 shows the dialogue box for editing the content of the portal. As you can see, it's very straightforward: choose to show or hide various

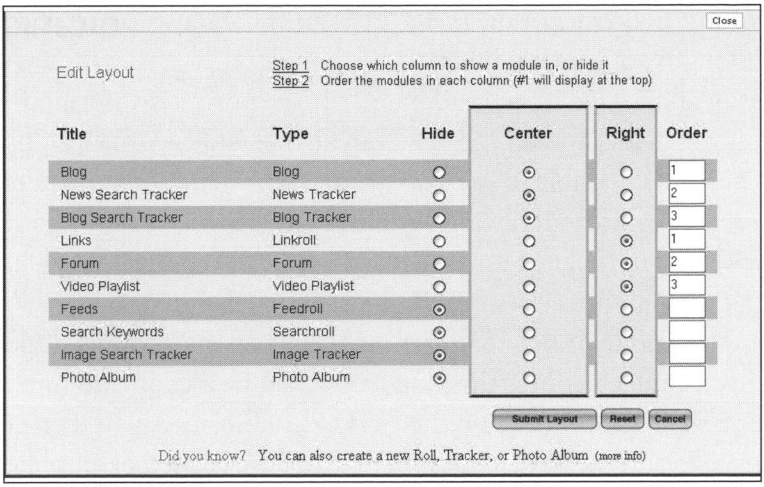

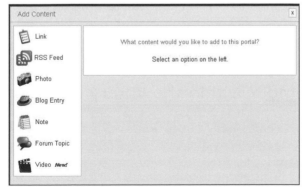

Figure 8.6 Editing the content of the Zimbio guide

options, and decide if they are to go into the main body of the page, in the right-hand side, and in what order they are to be displayed. It's very simple and intuitive, with the added bonus that if it all goes wrong it's easy to put everything back as it was.

Adding content modules is almost as simple, demonstrated by the dialogue box shown in Figure 8.7. Click on the appropriate module, follow the onscreen prompts and add in the content. Finally go back to

Figure 8.7 Adding content to a Zimbio portal

the editing content option (seen in Figure 8.6) and place your new content in an appropriate position.

The original owner or moderator of the portal is informed when changes are made, and an RSS feed can also be utilized for this purpose, so it's perfectly possible to keep up to date with alterations and additions to the resource without having to continually visit it.

The system is designed to allow members to add content as quickly and easily as possible, in a very similar fashion to that found in Squidoo. Zimbio provides a bookmarklet that can be added to the browser links bar. When you find a resource that you feel would be a good addition to the portal you can simply click on the 'Add to Zimbio' icon: you then choose the portal to add the page to (assuming you have created or are a member of several of them) and where you wish to add the new information, as seen in Figure 8.8.

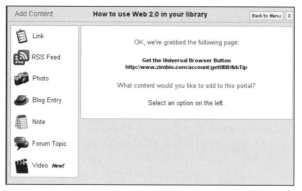

Copyright © 2007 Zimbio, Inc. Screen-shot reproduced with thanks.

Figure 8.8 Adding content via the Zimbio bookmarklet

Using Zimbio within the library or information centre

Zimbio has a number of features that allow the creators of a portal to open it out to more general use than is possible with something like Squidoo. While the basic concept is quite similar, with a focus on a particular subject area (call it a portal or call it a lens, it's still focused on one specific thing) there is a basic difference in the level of interaction possible.

The opportunities within Zimbio of having a weblog function open to any members to use, and the ease of creating a forum topic and allowing discussion back and forth, do facilitate the proper involvement of a community, where everyone can offer their own knowledge and insights into a specific area.

Of course, once you allow community involvement, that is exactly what you get, for good or ill. A portal that might start off looking at the intricacies of breeding Labrador dogs may quickly transmute into a discussion forum on looking after terriers, unless the moderator keeps a very close eye on the development of the forum. Of course at this point it might be thought necessary to establish a specific Squidoo lens for the former, and link to it from the latter. Inevitably a community is going to have different ideas and interests from those of the original designer; this is neither a good nor a bad thing, it's just the way of the world. If the moderator is too heavy-handed, this may discourage involvement and the community users may well disappear, and quite quickly at that.

In some circumstances a laissez-faire approach may be just what is needed – especially if the portal covers a subject area that is constantly changing, such as a sports team portal or a portal with a local community focus. It may therefore be worth spending a little time looking at existing portals in order to gain a deeper understanding of where and when they could be most useful. Some interesting ones to look at are:

- the New York Public Library at **www.zimbio.com/portal/New+York+Public+Library**
- the Institute of Museum and Library Services at **www.zimbio.com/portal/Institute+of+Museum+and+Library+Services**
- a day in the life of a librarian at **www.zimbio.com/portal/Day+in+the+life+of+a+librarian**
- distance learning at **www.zimbio.com/portal/Distance+Learning**
- Web 2.0 at **www.zimbio.com/portal/web+2.0**.

Other options

There are plenty of alternatives to the resources I've looked at in detail so far in this chapter. If you want to explore and try something different for yourself (and that's half the fun, of course) you may want to take a look at Boxxet at **http://boxxet.com/my/start.box**, which is designed to 'bring together the best of' a subject area by combining content from news, blogs, photographs and so on. Wetpaint at **www.wetpaint.com** is part weblog, part wiki (see below) and part website-authoring tool. Hubpages at **http://hubpages.com** is similar to Squidoo in that users can create their own content based on pre-existing modules. Fanpop at **www.fanpop.com** is a place for fans of a subject to collate data and share information, so this resource is probably best for discussions on pop groups or authors, rather than corporate use.

Wikis
An introduction

At the risk of simply confusing the situation further there is another alternative you may wish to consider if you're thinking of creating web page/site resources for your clients and users. This is a 'wiki', which is a type of website that allows, and in fact encourages, visitors to add, edit, change and hopefully improve on the existing content with the use of collaborative editing. Probably the best-known example of a wiki is the Wikipedia at **http://en.wikipedia.org**, and if you're wondering exactly what the word 'wiki' means, take a look at the explanation from the Wikipedia itself at **http://en.wikipedia.org/wiki/Wiki**.

The concept is very simple therefore – someone establishes a wiki on a subject that he or she is interested in, and other people either find it by serendipity or are invited, and they will add to the content. The growth of the wiki is dependent on the interests and enthusiasm of its members, and a dedicated, keen group of people can quickly produce a useful, accurate, almost 'living' document or creation. A major criticism of the concept of wikis is that individuals may, either deliberately or otherwise, include data that is incorrect, bringing the whole project into question. The usual response to such a criticism is that the community of users ensures that such inaccuracies do not remain in the wiki for long, as they are edited out by more knowledgeable or sharper-eyed contributors. Moreover, changes are always monitored, and previous versions are retained, so if there is any damage the wiki (or an individual page, which would be more likely) can be 'rolled back' to the previous version. Discussions can take place within the community on the addition of content, and issues and concerns can be flagged up for debate.

A great many different authoring tools are used to create a wiki, and the majority of these are actually embedded into the site – you don't have to download a product in order to create a wiki, you just need to be able to go to the site itself. Sometimes the tools are WYSIWYG ('what you see is what you get') and at other times the editing process is slightly more cumbersome, but in either case it is designed to be easier than creating web content using HTML. For example, Figure 8.9 demonstrates the editing screen for a Peanut Butter wiki (**http://pbwiki.com**).

Screen-shot taken December 2006 from PBwiki.com, used with permission.

Figure 8.9 The PBwiki editing system

While the PBwiki editing screen may initially look slightly daunting, the majority of options will be immediately familiar to most users of a word processor, and those icons which are unfamiliar are reasonably intuitive: of course if puzzlement continues a mouse rollover can banish any further confusion. Indeed, rather than having to start each page from scratch some tools provide some ready-made templates for users; Figure 8.10 shows another example from PBwiki.

Most creators of wikis usually make them available for everyone to see, although they may be kept private and restricted to a limited number of individuals. The owner(s) of the wiki can also decide who is allowed to edit the resource, so they keep overall control of it, but are able to identify and encourage users to grow the content without their direct intervention.

A wiki is sometimes likened to a content management system and it's true that there are similarities, although a CMS is generally to be found

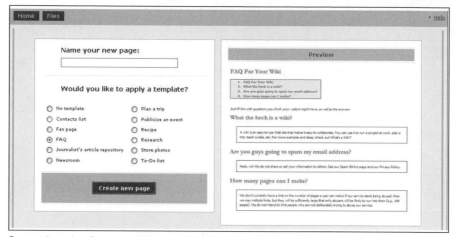

Screen-shot taken December 2006 from PBwiki.com, used with permission.

Figure 8.10 A PBwiki template

within an organization (rather than on the web itself) and it facilitates the needs of the organization, rather than perhaps having a specific focus on a subject area. A CMS will also by its very nature militate against input from just anyone, and will be strictly controlled in terms of content, users, templates and use. A wiki will tend to be within a slightly more 'relaxed' environment, but there is a grey area, so there are few hard and fast rules.

Wiki software

There are a large number of different types of software available for creating a wiki and, since most packages are free for basic use (with some charging a fee for some advanced services), it may be worth while exploring a variety of different resources before deciding on a package to use. The Wikipedia itself offers a comprehensive review of different tools at **http://en.wikipedia.org/wiki/Comparison_of_wiki_software**, or you can consult the WikiMatrix at **www.wikimatrix.org**, either of which will give you a dizzying array of options. You can make your task easier by narrowing down your options slightly while you are comparing different packages:

- Is it necessary to keep a page history to see who has changed what?
- Do you need to be able to roll back to a previous version?

- Are your intended users going to need a WYSIWYG system, or can they cope with a more advanced editing system?
- Do you want to host the software on your own system, or have it available directly on the web?
- Do you want to have a way of preventing spam being added automatically?
- Do you need templates, or do you prefer a 'go it alone' approach?
- Are you prepared to pay for the product and, if so, how much?

Now of course at this stage you probably have absolutely no idea about the answer to most of those questions (with the possible exception of the last one), so another step is to spend some time actually looking at wikis in order to see how they work, and perhaps to dip your toe into the water by adding some content or editing content if you feel confident enough to do so. Otherwise, just take a look at some examples. A good first port of call is the WikiIndex at **www.wikiindex.org/Welcome**, which lists a great many public wikis and is itself a wiki. Alternatively the WikiMedia site at **http://meta.wikimedia.org/wiki/Main_Page** lists some of the largest wikis in existence. However, if you prefer not to spend hours trawling through lists you might want to jump straight over to one or two of the following:

- Library 2.0 wiki at **http://wiki.library2.net/index.php/Main_Page**
  - 'serves the entire library community by bringing together a collection of resources about or relating to next-generation library services'
- Library Instruction wiki at **http://instructionwiki.org/Main_Page**
  - designed to be of use to librarians who are involved with or interested in instruction
- Library Success: a best practices wiki at **www.libsuccess.org**
  - designed to be a central repository of information on successful and innovative programmes
- Library and Information Science wiki at **http://liswiki.org/wiki/Main_Page**

- — intended to provide librarians and information professionals with a wiki to explore the usefulness of wikis
- ■ Blogging Libraries wiki at **www.blogwithoutalibrary.net/links/index.php?title=Welcome_to_the_Blogging_Libraries_Wiki**
  - — lists libraries that are running weblogs
- ■ AmbientLibrarian wiki at **www.ambientlibrarian.org/index.php?title=Main_Page**
  - — dedicated to helping information professionals learn more about Library 2.0
- ■ Shifted Librarian Presentation wiki at **http://theshiftedlibrarian.pbwiki.com**
  - — a collection of Jenny Levine's presentations in wiki format.

Of course, you may prefer simply to visit your preferred search engine and run a search for wikis in your subject area of interest.

Using a wiki

The previous examples should provide you with some ideas of what can be achieved with a wiki, but let's explore this in a little more detail. A wiki is worth using in a situation where you either have a group of people already, such as work colleagues or a community group, or where you can clearly identify people with an interest in a specific subject area. The wiki coverage needs to be broad enough to support the number of users who are involved, and vice versa. That is to say, if you intended to produce a general wiki like the Wikipedia it will require thousands of people to take part to add content and police the system. On the other hand, if you want to create a wiki that looks at the use of bandages in the American Civil War it is likely that only a small number of people will have any interest in that very specialized area. Consequently a balance is necessary, though to be fair it is likely that this is going to be self-regulating – a small number of people are not going to be able to produce an encyclopedia-sized wiki (unless they're very industrious), and if the subject of bandages in the civil war does touch a nerve then the community itself may decide to extend the subject content of the wiki to include other medical practices.

A second area that will affect the development of a wiki is currency of data. Wikis are very useful in situations where information changes on a regular basis, so they are particularly beneficial for subject guides, reading lists and discussion groups, conferences, information on sports teams or sporting events and so on. They are perhaps of less use in situations where information remains fairly static; if everyone agrees on a specific subject area then it may be more sensible to simply produce a more static HTML web page.

On the other hand, and at the risk of contradicting myself and confusing you, there may well be times when the importance of a wiki is less to do with the subject matter, and much more to do with the community group. The creation of a wiki could well be part of the development of a group of people; a wiki that was used to provide biographical details on members of staff would not change very often, but would be a really useful way of getting a new colleague involved, by having them write their own wiki page, linking it to others, and exploring interesting details on their new co-workers. Alternatively a wiki could be used as a focal point to bring together a group of people who otherwise would never have identified each other.

Yet another reason to use a wiki would be in a situation where the users have less interest in how content is created than in the content itself; learning HTML is not always the easiest thing to do and can be time consuming. If individuals are more interested in getting their content and 'voice' heard, having to create HTML web pages may well put them off to the point where nothing is created. A wiki, with its simplified editing format, should not prove to be an obstacle or distraction. It would be wrong therefore to simply focus on one aspect of a wiki, since the creation of one will potentially have a number of quite far-reaching effects.

It is also important to consider why it may be a bad idea to create a wiki. If you are unable to trust your audience to act sensibly and in the best interests of the wiki it may be wise to consider other options. For example, there are some contentious subjects about which people feel very strongly, and they wish to get their viewpoint across, perhaps at the expense of differing views. They may be prepared to sit and re-edit a page every single time someone adds or changes content they disagree with. This leads to a back-and-forth battle that achieves very little, or in order to keep the peace the owner of the wiki may feel that it is necessary to 'lock' a page so that it cannot be edited and have a very bland statement on the page that satisfies no one. If the wiki is going to cover a wide subject area it may be necessary to do considerable work in the background to create a structure for the wiki – template pages for different subject areas, navigation aids and so on. While this doesn't necessarily mean that you shouldn't use a wiki, you have to be realistic, and if it is going to be very time-consuming for all concerned then perhaps other options should be considered.

A lens, a portal or a wiki?

I suppose I could also add to this heading 'or a weblog?', since all these resources provide different ways of producing content quickly and relatively simply. There is no 'one size fits all' solution, nor is there a 'if x then y' answer, and sometimes one or more options would work perfectly well. I think the important point is to be less concerned with the actual technology, and more interested in the end result; decide what you want to achieve first, and then the solution should become obvious – or at least a little clearer. If you start by looking at the resource first, and try to shoehorn that into what you want to do, failure will almost certainly be the outcome. Rather, you need to think about what you wish to achieve, and then see what resource, or type of resource will best enable you to do that.

If your major concern is to provide an outlet for your own 'voice' or opinion, then clearly a weblog has to be a good approach, since you control everything that goes into the weblog, and (unless you operate a multi-author weblog) overall control is absolute. On the other hand, you may want to promote yourself as an expert in a particular area, in which case a Squidoo list may be rather more sensible, and of course you could always have a link directly to your own weblog as well, to give both of them a little boost.

At the other end of the spectrum, community involvement allows for a richness that will be missing from a weblog or lens, and it also ensures that more information can be made available, with everyone in the group being able to contribute to the growth of the resource. A portal will enable a group dynamic to thrive, with opportunities for discussion inherent in a joint weblog and forum, while a wiki will concentrate more on what a group can create, so the focus will be rather different there.

Currency is another issue that should be included in the mix. A weblog or lens can be updated virtually instantaneously, so they are both good ways of dealing with and manipulating data. You will probably find that the portal or wiki approach is not going to be as fast, and it is quite possible that someone could add a page to a wiki that isn't viewed or edited by anyone for months, if at all. So, if the main interest is a repository of information, a portal or wiki may work well. On the other hand, a weblog can be an excellent way of gathering together, over a period of time, a repository of information on a particular subject.

Is it important to get information out to people quickly? If so, then obviously a weblog is going to be the perfect mechanism for that, and the RSS feed can work in conjunction with readers' news aggregators to ensure that speed of service. One could equally argue that the other resources could provide something similar by having an RSS feed associated with them. On the whole, however, if speed is an issue, a weblog approach would have to be a front runner.

Accuracy and trustworthiness is another key area to consider. I neither expect nor necessarily require a weblog to give me information that is 100% accurate. I know that a weblog and a lens will be a reflection of the interests and biases of its author(s), and I can take that into account when using the information provided. However, if I need information that is checked and has a higher 'trustworthy' element to it, a portal or specific wiki would be the place I would go. Having said that, I'm also aware that it is just as easy to write a biased piece of work in a portal or wiki, and there have been lots of examples of this with resources such as the Wikipedia. It could, however, be argued that, in relative terms, a community resource will be checked, edited and corrected on a more regular basis than a weblog or lens. This does not negate the rule that any information found in any resource should be checked against another source.

Conclusion

All the utilities mentioned in this chapter allow users to create an entirely different set of resources to those they could have done previously. It has been argued that Web 2.0 is merely old wine in new bottles, and I have a certain sympathy with that view. However, one could argue that about the internet itself, and to take it to ridiculous extremes there isn't that much in conceptual difference between creating a web page and writing on a slate – they're both ways of capturing and publishing content.

The important point is that it is becoming so much easier to publish information, and we're now moving into a situation where the technology is becoming almost irrelevant, as users do not need to know anything about web-page creation, HTML or any other technical issues. If someone, or a group of people, has a message they want to publish it is increasingly easy to do so. Moreover, the speed of the creation of that message and its delivery is simply getting faster with each passing day.

As information professionals we are less and less 'gatekeepers' of information, firstly storing it and then retrieving it on demand for users, but rather 'facilitators' in helping our user communities to utilize the tools for themselves.

URLs mentioned in this chapter

www.ambientlibrarian.org/index.php?title=Main_Page
www.blogwithoutalibrary.net/links/index.php?title=Welcome_to_the_
    Blogging_Libraries_Wiki
http://boxxet.com/my/start.box
http://del.icio.us
http://en.wikipedia.org
http://en.wikipedia.org/wiki/Comparison_of_wiki_software
http://en.wikipedia.org/wiki/Wiki
www.fanpop.com
www.flickr.com
http://hubpages.com
http://instructionwiki.org/Main_Page
www.libsuccess.org
http://liswiki.org/wiki/Main_Page
http://maps.google.com
http://meta.wikimedia.org/wiki/Main_Page
www.pbwiki.com

www.squidoo.com.

www.squidoo.com/exeterpubliclibrary

www.squidoo.com/library20

www.squidoo.com/librarytricks

www.squidoo.com/LIS701Dom

www.squidoo.com/LISAHELP

www.squidoo.com/monitorlinks

www.squidoo.com/opac

www.squidoo.com/State_Library_of_Pennsylvania

www.squidoo.com/web2inyourlibrary

http://theshiftedlibrarian.pbwiki.com

www.wetpaint.com

http://wiki.library2.net/index.php/Main_Page

www.wikiindex.org/Welcome

www.wikimatrix.org

www.zimbio.com

www.zimbio.com/portal/Day+in+the+life+of+a+librarian

www.zimbio.com/portal/Distance+Learning

www.zimbio.com/portal/Institute+of+Museum+and+Library+Services

www.zimbio.com/portal/New+York+Public+Library

www.zimbio.com/portal/web+2.0

Chapter 9

Using instant messaging

Introduction

When people talk about the internet they will often highlight different things: a technical person will talk happily for hours about different standards and program languages; a librarian will refer to all the useful information and databases available to users; a salesperson will indicate how much money can be made using it and so on. For all these people the key element of the internet is different, but in actual fact what brings all of these different things together is one thing – people talking to other people. It's too easy to forget that this is really the key element, and without people talking to each other the internet doesn't actually amount to much.

There are of course lots of ways in which people can talk to each other – by producing a web page to act as their poster, saying whatever they choose, or by communicating via bulletin board, e-mail and so forth. Instant messaging, where people are able to type out a message and instantly send it to someone else who can read it in real time and then respond, is by no means a new addition to the internet – it has been around in various forms for quite some time. However, with the advent of Web 2.0 resources people are looking at this with fresh eyes, and some libraries are exploring the ways in which it can be used within their systems.

This chapter looks at instant messaging in more depth in order to give readers a much clearer indication of what it is and how they may be able to use it themselves.

What is instant messaging?

Instant messaging, or IM, is a form of real-time, virtually instantaneous communication between two or more people using a textual format. IM software allows the participants to communicate via a small text-box on the screen, and the resource displays the textual communication all parties have made. Most packages will let users indicate if they are online or offline by way of a status alert (such as 'busy', 'at lunch' or 'away'), and these packages can be turned on or off as appropriate. Some resources will also allow people to share a search, participate in a video chat, use audio or send/receive files. An IM conversation may be as short as a couple of lines of text swopped back and forth between participants, or it could be a very long, in-depth discussion. Participants could be connected for several hours without saying anything, each simply keeping their chat windows open so, unlike a telephone call or e-mail, an IM discussion can take place over several hours, involving various different formats of data.

IM communication tends to be fairly informal, with a high emphasis on short abbreviations such as IMO (in my opinion), bbiab (be back in a bit) or the unpronounceable ROFLMAO (rolling on the floor laughing my ass off). Emoticons – small icons used to demonstrate pleasure, sadness, confusion and so on – are often widely used as well. Communication is less intrusive than a telephone call, and certainly quieter! At the choice of the user, the conversation(s) can be kept and stored or they may be transient in nature.

In order for IM to take place in most cases it is necessary to have a client installed on the computer you're using. There are resources that do not absolutely require that, but for the time being we'll concentrate on looking at the basics. This chapter will also cover the ways in which IM can be used within a library setting, and a few of the advantages and disadvantages inherent in such a system. Figure 9.1 shows an IM conversation taking place using Microsoft Messenger.

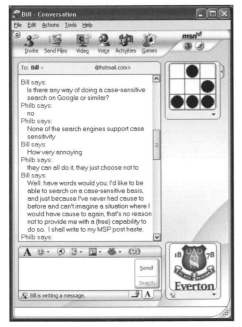

Screen-shot reproduced with thanks.

Figure 9.1 A conversation between two people using MSN Messenger

What software is needed?

There are a lot of different packages available that let people IM. In fact, you may already have such a package on your own computer, and if you use Windows you will almost certainly have MSN Messenger available to you. If you prefer to use Microsoft products you can get more information on it, and download a free copy, at **http://get.live.com/ messenger/ overview**. Installation is very straightforward, and you can sign into the system by using an e-mail address and password. Alternatively, if you are first and foremost a Yahoo! user, then you can obtain Yahoo! Messenger at **http://messenger. yahoo.com**. If you use AOL (or in fact even if you don't subscribe to AOL, you can still use their system) you might want to consider AOL Instant Messenger (AIM), at **http://info.aol.co.uk/aim** if you are based in the UK, or go to the international site at **www.aim.com**. On the other hand, if you make a lot of use of Google, and in particular its e-mail system Gmail, you may wish to consider using that, available at **www.google.com/talk**.

Your choice of system is important because, unlike a telephone, you are limited to being able to speak to people who are using the same system, though once again it's necessary to qualify that, since there are one or two packages that we'll look at later which overcome this problem. Of course, there is nothing to stop you downloading, installing and using all these resources on your own system, although if you are new to the entire concept I suggest choosing just one to begin with.

If you're rather more experienced at IM, however, you might wish to go for a client that supports a variety of different systems, and there are once again plenty of these to look at. Trillian at **www.ceruleanstudios.com/learn** supports all the major IM clients, as well as various other similar chat systems such as ICQ and IRC. Gaim at **http://gaim.sourceforge.net** is a package that works with various clients and operating systems and some corporate messaging systems such as Novell GroupWise Messenger. If you use a Mac operating system you might be more interested in Fire, available at **http://fire.sourceforge.net**. Finally, and just to add to the confusion of options a little more, if you prefer not to install anything onto your own computer or system (and, as a word of warning right at the outset, opposition to IM is often based on the idea of downloading software onto a computer when it may not be safe to do so), it's worth looking at Meebo, which you can find at **http://wwwl.meebo.com/index-en.html**.

When you are installing the software, you will usually be asked to fill out a profile, with details of who you are, where you live, phone numbers and so on. It's really not necessary to include this type of information – certainly not as a private individual, although if you decide to use IM as one of your library resources you may find it helpful to input information about the library instead.

There is no one system that is better than any other, so as well as trying out one or two packages you might want to ask friends and colleagues what system(s) they use, and then focus on the most popular to start you off, though it's worth reiterating that in the longer term you'll want to be able to communicate across the board, either by providing a multiplicity of IM clients, or by concentrating on one of the resources mentioned above. My personal preference is MSN Messenger, and if you want to try the system out please feel free to add me as a contact using my philb@philb.com e-mail address.

It's a good idea not to transmit any kind of sensitive data – although it's unlikely that your communication is going to be intercepted, it is possible, at least in theory. Indeed, some systems, such as MSN Messenger, explicitly advise at the beginning of each chat session that you should not pass on credit-card details and so on. While it is possible to send and receive files, unless you know and trust the person you are talking to, this is unwise, since IM clients do not automatically check for viruses as do e-mail packages, and it is all too easy to end up with a virus on your system. Similarly, do not click on any hyperlinks that are included in an IM message as they may also be unsafe. It is also always worth making sure that you have the most up-to-date version of the IM client – although the software is going to be of a high quality (especially if you choose one of the packages mentioned in this chapter), it is always being improved, and new security features are being added.

Using IM in a library setting
Reference query work

An obvious way of using IM within a library context is to provide immediate access to library staff, in particular the reference services. Dozens of libraries around the world are already using IM for exactly this purpose, and a good listing of them can be found at the Library Success best practices wiki at **http://libsuccess.org/index.php?title=Libraries_ Using_IM_Reference**. IM works in the same way that any other text-based communication works, and in fact you could think of it just as a speedier way of conducting a reference query via e-mail, although according to Aaron Schmidt and Michael Stephens (IM Me, *Library Journal*, 1 April 2005, **www.libraryjournal.com/article/CA512192.html**) a commonly asked introductory question is 'Are you real or are you a robot?'

IM has a number of advantages and disadvantages over traditional reference query answering. The query is there on the screen for both parties to see and it doesn't disappear in general conversation. Of course, just because it can be seen on the screen doesn't mean that it is clear: 'Can you give me information about race relations in Georgia?' doesn't specify if the enquirer means the American state or the country neighbouring Russia.

Another important point is that when you create your account, and publicize it, people will then be able to add your details to their own profile, so they will be reminded of your existence every time they log onto their IM client (which generally happens whenever they start their computer), or when you log on yourself. That is a constant presence that you, your library and your service have on someone else's desktop; it's almost like sitting next to someone while they work, ready to help them out whenever they need assistance, without the necessity for them to break off from what they're currently doing. And IM is no longer limited to the desktop computer: many PDAs (personal digital assistants) now come with software that includes IM functionality. Couldn't the user simply ring up the enquiry or reference desk? Well, yes, they could, but a reply via IM will be more helpful, giving content that can be cut and pasted into another application, or links that can be used while on the run, so in fact it's a far more flexible system.

Running searches

IM can be used to run searches, in specific situations. For example, the Microsoft Encarta encyclopedia has an IM interface, and if you add Encarta@botmetro.net to your list of contacts you can open up a reference session and query the encyclopedia without reference to your browser.

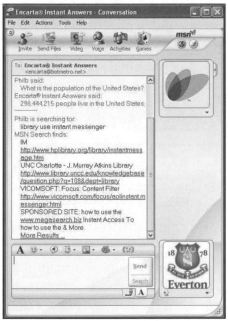

Figure 9.2 shows a 'conversation' of this nature, in which I asked for the population of the USA.

It is also possible to run a search from any conversation window (this is not a feature specific to Encarta). Simply type in the search term(s) as appropriate and click on the 'Search' button. This then sends the query to Microsoft's search engine, which then sends back a response. This can be useful if you are in discussions with a user, and want to check a fact or obtain a URL quickly, since in 'their' IM dialogue window they will see you asking the questions and the URLs that are returned as well.

Figure 9.2 Using IM for reference enquiry work

Consequently, it is very easy to take the whole concept of search, and plug it into a completely different resource without any difficulty at all. By the way, in case you are wondering, the images to the right of the dialogue box in Figure 9.2 are the avatars used to identify the individuals taking part in the conversation. These can be personalized, using a Microsoft icon, in the case of Encarta, or a photograph or any other image – such as a favourite football team badge, as in my case.

Contacting colleagues

IM can be a very effective alternative to e-mail, if for no other reason than it is instant. Rather than write an e-mail, send it, wait for it to arrive in the colleague's in tray, then wait for them to read it and finally respond to you, it may actually be more effective to simply IM the same person and say 'How is 3 pm for you?' If you and your colleagues are spread out over a wide distance, which may be several floors, different buildings or indeed different continents, IM provides another communication option and trivial queries that would otherwise go by e-mail can sit quite happily in an IM window until the recipient can get around to responding. It may also be considerably cheaper to send an IM than to make a phone call.

Without wishing to travel too far down this particular route, some staff may feel more comfortable discussing various issues informally, without the need to use e-mail, but equally without having to meet face to face.

Some do's and don'ts

Since all IM software gives users the ability to set their status ('away', 'busy' and so on) it's important to use these – it can be very frustrating for users if they attempt to open a discussion with a contact and wait for ages before realizing, or more likely having to assume, that the person on the other end of the message is away from their desk or perhaps taking a call.

Typing accuracy is not a priority. The important thing to remember with IM is that it is informal, and the point of the exercise is to transmit the required information as quickly as possible – so don't spend too much time checking for typos unless either the sense or accuracy of the information being made available is at stake. Users of IM are going to be far less bothered or concerned by minor errors than they would be in an e-mail response or a hard-copy reply to a query.

While speed is important, you should not feel that you are being rushed to deliver a response. This is far more difficult to assess in an IM setting than when using other methods – in a face-to-face interview the enquirer can see you moving from one reference book to another trying to track down the answer, and even on the phone they may be able to hear you flicking through a book. With IM that simply doesn't happen, so it makes good sense to pop back every few minutes to say 'I'm still looking!', which is all that the enquirer needs to remain part of the conversation.

Accept that informal communication can still be effective communication. The majority of people who use the IM service you can provide will almost certainly be using it for communication with friends and colleagues, and will be happier with informal discussions. In fact, starting a discussion with 'Good afternoon. How may I be of assistance to you with respect to any queries that you may have for us today?' is probably going to put people off: far better to start by saying 'Hi, my name's Phil and I'm the reference librarian – how can I help?' Also, don't be afraid of using abbreviations, since it may not only help put the enquirer at their ease, but it can save keystrokes and time.

Don't forget that while it is possible to provide information electronically, either by providing a link to a resource or offering a file for download, there will still be times when an enquirer will have to come into the library in order to get their query answered.

Concerns over using IM in a library setting

For many people the idea of using IM is a real challenge, particularly if they have never been exposed to that type of communication before. It's therefore necessary to spend some time training people on how to use the system to best advantage. Ideally include the use of IM in other training sessions being run for staff, and emphasize the basics of responding, inserting URLs, sending files and so on. It's also a good idea to run practice sessions as well.

Another concern may be that the reference librarian will end up with several IM queries at once, but this need not be a problem – the solution lies in the status message option. If you have enough queries to be going on with, simply change status to 'Busy' or something similar, deal with any further requests with a 'Please come back in 10 minutes' response, and then change the status again once the rush has calmed down.

Some people are simply not adept at using a keyboard, or they may feel that their typing speed isn't up to scratch. This can be particularly evident when faced with someone at the other end of the query who seems able to type at 100 words a minute and who wants or is expecting an almost instantaneous answer. Once again, this need not be an issue – typing speed may well improve with increased use of the keyboard, or a typing course can be arranged. An impatient user would be the same if they were on the telephone or in a face-to-face situation, and the same methods used to respond in those situations can be employed just as effectively in an IM setting – the librarian is still the one who is (or should be) in control of the situation, and they should not allow themselves to be bullied.

There may be concerns about receiving files via IM that have not been virus checked. A solution that may satisfy the technical support staff may be to use a package such as Meebo that doesn't need to be downloaded or installed onto a system, but can simply be used as another web-based resource. This is the route that a lot of librarians are taking, and in fact Meebo cites the fact that librarians are one of its most loyal user groups in its weblog at **http://blog.meebo.com/?p=240**. There are various other chat resources that can be employed (mentioned in Chapter 3 on weblogs) which allow a library to run an IM service without any downloading issues at all. If concerns persist, software such as ChatPatrol, available from **www.chatpatrol.com**, that can monitor IM discussions for viruses (as well as providing other security measures) may well be an answer.

Another response to the 'danger' of allowing IM facilities within a library setting is to point out that a lot of systems, such as MySpace, already have a feature in place that will almost certainly get around any restrictions that the library has, and if IM is not in use, or worse is banned, all that it does is to show that the library isn't keeping up to date with technological advances. We're currently moving from a situation where having IM resources makes the library look as though it knows what is going on and is keeping up to date to the point where not having IM available will show up the library service as being behind the times.

It may be argued that IM is a fad or toy used only by teenagers. This argument should have no part to play in a public library situation where teenagers are a user group that should be encouraged, but it may in theory have more force within a corporate environment. However, a report by Pew Internet/American Life in 2004 (**www.pewinternet.org/ pdfs/PIP_Instantmessage_Report.pdf**) reported that 53 million Americans were using IM and 24% were doing more IM than e-mail. Doubtless this figure has increased since the report was published.

Using web-based chat systems

It is worth spending just a few moments looking at a variation of IM, although it could easily be argued that it is an entirely different system, and that is web-based chat. In principle this and IM are very similar, in that users can chat to librarians in real time in a textual format using a keyboard and software. Web-based chat, however, requires different software, and leads to a rather more sophisticated set-up.

Enquirers go to a specific page on the library site, such as California's AskNow service at **www.asknow.org**, and connect with a librarian to seek an answer to their information requirements. The software allows the librarian to 'push' pages to an enquirer, 'co-browse' where both are able to view the same page, and save the chat session for later use if necessary. The software required for these services can be expensive, both in terms of cost and computer power. However, an advantage of this type of service is that libraries have been able to join together to provide a unified enquiry service which can span a large geographic area. A good overview of the difference between these services and those offered by IM systems is provided by Sarah Houghton-Jan in an article entitled Virtual Reference @ Your Library, available at **www.ala.org/ala/aasl/aaslpubsandjournals/ kqweb/kqarchives/v33/333Houghton.htm**.

Implementing an IM system

Hopefully you will be interested or intrigued enough to consider trying IM for reference work within your own organization. One obvious approach is simply to download and install an IM client, then advertise it, perhaps on your website, or via posters or a newsletter, and see what happens – the 'just do it' approach. While this has a number of merits, mainly that you can try out something with limited involvement from the powers that be, if a service is going to be taken seriously it does need to be well thought out, because if your users become disillusioned it will be very hard, perhaps impossible, to win them back. Consequently it is worth doing a little pre-planning.

Which system?

As seen earlier in this chapter, there are various options available to you, with no clear choice between them. It is probably worth asking around to see if there is a resource that most of your clients and colleagues are already using (or, more likely, their sons and daughters), and don't forget to talk to staff in your technical support department – if anyone is using IM it's almost certainly going to be them. While you're talking to them, raise the potential spectre of installing IM software on various machines and gauge the possibility of doing this in inverse proportion to the look of horror on their faces. It may be necessary at that point to go down the route of having a chat box installed onto either your weblog or a web page.

What will you offer, and to whom?

It's important to be clear before you start a service on the limitations and boundaries of the service. You need to be able to answer all the following questions to your own satisfaction before the service goes live in any meaningful way:

- *When will the service be available?*
  Will an information professional be on call from 9 a.m. to 5 p.m., or just for specific periods of time, such as every afternoon, or will it be an ad hoc system?
- *Who is going to be responsible for answering queries?*
  Are staff going to take turns? Is it going to be the responsibility of the individual who is already on the reference desk? Is it going to be necessary to put a rota in place? Will your system allow members of staff to create a status message suggesting that users contact someone else if they are busy?
- *What type of queries are you going to answer?*
  Will this range from the address of the library through to catalogue

searches, or will only quick reference queries be covered?

■ *Who is the service for?*
Is it just for members of your organization, or for anyone who contacts you? If it's the former, how is this policy going to be implemented – how can someone 'prove' they have a right to use the system?

■ *Are you going to send files to enquirers?*
— Some queries may be answered by sending the user a file: who takes responsibility for ensuring that no virus is attached, and how will that be made clear to the enquirer?

■ *How long are you prepared to spend on an enquiry?*
— If the user is unable to wait for an answer, what process is going to be put in place to get the answer to them?

The infrastructure

Obviously staff will need to be trained on the use of the system, so this must be planned in advance. Not only will they need to know the technical basics of how the service works and to demonstrate a competency in using IM, such as knowing how to insert links to assist in enquiry answering, but they'll need to know what is expected of them in terms of communication skills.

What, if any, information regarding the communication is going to be stored, and what purpose is it going to be put to? There will obviously be a desire to keep details on IM queries – what times prove to be busiest and on what days, for example, simply so that it's possible to ensure coverage of an IM service, but is it desirable to keep details of the questions that are asked, or the answers given? You probably won't want to keep personal details of who is asking for assistance, but you may want to differentiate between staff and external users, for example. How are you going to be able to reliably gather that data?

There should also be a clear written policy on the use of IM within the library setting – a good base to work from is the American Library Association Guidelines for Implementing and Maintaining Virtual Reference Services available at **www.ala.org/ala/rusa/rusaprotools/referenceguide/ virtrefguidelines.htm**.

Promotion of IM services

For any service to succeed, people need to know about it: how they can use it, when it's available, what they can expect from the service and also what is expected of them. Failure to properly publicize the service will lead to almost certain failure of the service itself, so it's worth taking time to look at all the different promotion methods you can use. For example:

- details on the website itself
- details in the weblog
- IM details on business cards
- IM details on official library stationery
- mentions in any library newsletters
- information on posters within the library
- details made available to new members of staff
- mentions in any induction programmes.

Case study: Marin County Library and instant messaging

Sarah Houghton-Jan is the Information and Web Services Manager for the San Mateo County Library in California. Sarah is also a member of the California Library Association's Assembly and of LITA (Library and Information Technology Association)'s Top Technology Trends Committee. She presents physically and virtually at many conferences and library events each year on libraries and technology.

Sarah is the author of LibrarianInBlack at **http://librarianinblack. typepad.com** and she has published in a number of library and technology trade publications. She was previously employed by the Marin County Free Library and is looking at using instant messaging from the viewpoint of both the time she spent using IM within the library, but also from her personal and extensive knowledge and experience of using IM.

Q: Can you tell me a little about the library?

A: The Marin County Free Library website is at
http://co.marin.ca.us/library and it also has a weblog at
www.marincountyfreelibrary.blogspot.com. Physically it is
based in California, USA.

Q: Why did you decide to try using IM?

A: We saw that our statistics for our web-based chat
service, which was statewide at that time, were relatively
low given our population. We also saw that students and
working adults in our community were using instant
messaging to communicate with each other. I attended an
inspiring session at an Internet Librarian conference a few
years ago, presented by Michael Stephens and Aaron
Schmidt, about using IM for reference services, and I was
sold. As the e-Services Librarian, I introduced the idea to
staff and they were sold on it too.

Q: How long have you been using it?

A: MCFL's project is three years old now and doing well, or
so I am told. [Sarah has since moved to another position in
another library.]

Q: Do you have a preferred client?

A: I personally prefer Trillian, at **www.ceruleanstudios.com**,
since it runs in the system tray and has a number of features
and customization options that work well for libraries. Others
prefer Gaim at **http://gaim.sourceforge.net** for other reasons.
Meebo at **http://wwwl.meebo.com/index-en.html** is also
absolutely fabulous, especially given the MeeboMe widget
(**www.meebome.com/?o**) which allows anyone to
anonymously chat with the librarian via a box placed on any
web page.

Q: Did you need to get anyone's permission to do it?

A: Yes, we needed to get permission from both the county's
IT department and the library's administration.

Q: How integral is it to the reference work in the library?

A: IM reference complements the other forms of reference

the library offers: e-mail, phone, in-person and web-based chat. I felt that we were reaching a whole new audience with IM, though – individuals who would not use our other reference service options.

Q: How popular is the service – do you have any feeling for who uses it most, young/old, etc.?

A: The statistics were quite good at MCFL up to the time of my departure. I'm not sure what they're like now. We had a large distribution of users, age-wise. We got middle and high schoolers needing homework help, but quite a few adults IMing us during the workday wanting research help for their work, to place items on hold, etc. I would say the under-18/over-18 users were split 50/50.

Q: Any particular type of enquiries, or a complete mishmash?

A: Via IM we got the same type of questions you would get via any other reference medium. The one difference is that the troubleshooting questions we got (for databases, the catalogue, e-books) were often by more advanced users – people who had already tried the basics. To me this reflected that IM users were, overall, more tech-savvy than our other reference medium users.

Q: How does the service work – what I mean is, someone pops up with an IM query, does the member of staff then set status to busy while the question is answered, or can they multi-task with more than one query at a time?

A: Staff would multi-task with multiple queries if they came up, but it was rare for more than one question to come in at a time.

Q: Do the library staff each have an IM account, and is there another for the quick reference work?

A: There was one set screen name for reference enquiries, and staff had a separate IM network set up to talk with each other, one that was not interoperable with the IM service used for reference.

Q: Do you use the IM client to send files, etc. to answer a question? Would you accept files via IM?

A: No, we turned off file-sharing for security purposes.

Q: Do you get inappropriate messages? (Not specifically rude ones, but spam, etc.)

A: We did get inappropriate messages, and developed scripts to help staff deal with them. We found that the number dropped off after the first few months . . . kind of like kids prank-calling to see how far they could push us, and then getting bored with it pretty quickly when we didn't take the bait.

Q: Do you keep statistics?

A: Yes, we did. I don't know if they are still doing that.

Q: Are you happy with the way the service works, or do you want to/intend to make changes?

A: What I would like is for an IM aggregator, like Trillian, Meebo or Gaim, to be able to allow multiple people to monitor one screen name – to allow an IM co-operative to be established locally, statewide or nationwide. The addition of a feature like this is hugely key to IM becoming more widespread among libraries.

Q: What advice would you give an information centre that is thinking of trying out an IM service?

A: Read some of the many articles and blog posts written on IM reference best practices. Contact some of the libraries currently offering the service to ask specific questions about implementing the service. Get staff on board first and give the participating librarians plenty of time to practise before launch. Advertise it everywhere students and tech-savvy people hang out in your community – restaurants, skate parks, grocery stores, movie theatres – everywhere you can think of.

Conclusion

Instant messaging is a resource that has swiftly become fully established and accepted within the wider internet community. It is widely used by many different groups of people, though admittedly with a slight emphasis towards teenage users; a rather depressing (albeit apocryphal) comment I've heard mentioned is 'e-mail is for old people' as most students are using IM and SMS text services to communicate.

IM allows the library or information service to continue outreach work with groups of users who may otherwise never set foot into the library. By utilizing these services the information service not only continues to remain relevant in the 21st century, but it's indicating very graphically, on every desktop of every user every day, that it still has an important part to play in the professional provision of information.

URLs mentioned in this chapter

www.aim.com

www.ala.org/ala/aasl/aaslpubsandjournals/kqweb/kqarchives/v33/
333Houghton.htm

www.ala.org/ala/rusa/rusaprotools/referenceguide/virtrefguidelines.htm

www.asknow.org

http://blog.meebo.com/?p=240

www.ceruleanstudios.com

www.ceruleanstudios.com/learn

www.chatpatrol.com

http://co.marin.ca.us/library

http://fire.sourceforge.net

http://gaim.sourceforge.net

http://get.live.com/messenger/overview

www.google.com/talk

http://info.aol.co.uk/aim

http://librarianinblack.typepad.com

www.libraryjournal.com/article/CA512192.html

http://libsuccess.org/index.php?title=Libraries_Using_IM_Reference

www.marincountyfreelibrary.blogspot.com

http://messenger.yahoo.com

http://wwwl.meebo.com/index-en.html

www.meebome.com/?o

www.pewinternet.org/pdfs/PIP_Instantmessage_Report.pdf

Chapter 10
Photograph-sharing utilities

Introduction

Long before many people were aware of Web 2.0, photograph-sharing sites were appearing on the web. With the advent of digital cameras, both of the point-and-snap variety and more professional digital SLR cameras, not to mention cameras on mobile phones, there has been an explosion of photography, with the attendant wish to be able to share those photographs with friends and family.

This is not a hard thing to do, and in relative terms is quite straightforward; the users of the system are the ones supplying the content, so they simply need somewhere to upload their photographs and a method of doing so. But there is little point or interest in just putting a lot of photographs online, and expecting people to go through them in an electronic version of viewing holiday snaps. Since the medium is electronic, photographs can be described, put into a set, or indeed into several different sets and commented upon. One of the first utilities that provided this added value was Flickr (**www.flickr.com**). It isn't of course the only one, but it is one of the better known ones, and is representative of all the photo-sharing resources.

Flickr

To describe Flickr as a photograph-sharing and management resource is rather like calling the Empire State Building a structure; while it may be strictly speaking correct it doesn't even hint at the size of the resource that is available. The strength of Flickr lies in its social community aspect, with participants working together to create many different 'pools' of photographs, and tagging them for easy location and identification. Without this added element Flickr would indeed be a place that individuals could use to post photographs onto the web and tell their friends about them so that they could view them, although to be fair it's certainly true that many people do exactly that, and they're happy to limit their involvement with Flickr to that level of participation. However, by allowing users to share resources and to collaborate with each other, much more can be achieved.

Utilizing Flickr as an information resource

The creation of 'groups' or 'pools' of photographs is one simple and basic way of sharing information about a subject – be it something tangible such as New York City or Big Ben, or something rather more esoteric such as depictions of the number 9 in different guises. There are also groups for people who wish to improve their photography, who post photographs for others to comment on, while they comment in turn on other people's works. Consequently Flickr can be a useful resource for obtaining photographic information about a subject. Should I need to know what a Mongolian yurt looks like, I can quickly type the terms into the Flickr search box (**www.flickr.com/search**) and I'm immediately presented with over 90 images. It's fair to say that some of those are not on topic, since some of the images returned are of a rock band, or photographs of sheep, but the vast majority of them do give me a very clear idea of what these structures look like, and moreover indicate just how many different types there are. I could run a search on one of the major image search engines just as easily, and Google provides me with over four times the number of images.

The Flickr search feature is very basic, limiting searches to your own photographs, those of your contacts or everyone's, with a search on tags or full text. The advanced feature (**www.flickr.com/search/advanced**) is rather more useful as it allows the choice of searching for all words, any words or the exact phrase on full text or tags. It is also possible to exclude particular words. A second option allows searchers to limit the search according to the date the photographs were taken or posted. Flickr is working with Creative Commons (**www.flickr.com/ creativecommons**) so that searchers can limit searches to photographs tagged with a Creative Commons licence to use commercially, or to modify and adapt.

There are a number of differences between the traditional image search engine (or traditional search engine with image search bolted onto it) and Flickr. Firstly the images are much more personalized: they are not publicity stills, or advertising images - they have been taken by individuals who have an interest in that specific subject matter, and while this is obviously an issue of personal taste, the images are often much more interesting and informative because of this. Secondly it's possible to view other photographs by the same photographer - they may have created their own 'set' of photographs of Mongolian yurts or, more likely, a rather broader set of images of Mongolia, or yurts from around the world.

If a researcher has an interest in one specific aspect of a subject, they may find it helpful or interesting to be able to broaden or narrow their search according to the sets produced by that photographer. The tags used to identify or describe photographs may also prove to be helpful to researchers by suggesting terms they may not have thought of themselves prior to starting their research. The Flickr interface makes it very easy to click on another tag in order to run a second search. Importantly the search function does not simply return another set of images, rather it clusters images together. Consequently a search on the tag 'Mongolia' returns four different clusters of images, which in turn concentrate on horses and the nomadic way of life, China and intercontinental travel, the Gobi desert, and temples and monasteries. Finally one last collection of images is for those that have recently been uploaded (very often the same day as the search), so it really is very easy to keep current with what is being published.

Links

Some Flickr groups provide immediate links to other websites or information resources. For example, some of the groups that deal with recipes will illustrate delightful dishes, and the photographer will then link to the site (perhaps their own, perhaps not) that provides the recipe.

Speed

This immediacy allows for other functionality that traditional resources are unable to match. Posting images onto Flickr is an almost instantaneous event: once a photograph has been taken it can be uploaded in a matter of seconds, then tagged and added to an appropriate group. Traditional image search engines cannot compete with Flickr in terms of speed, since they need to continually spider web pages for new images, retrieve them, include them in their databases and make them available, which can take days or weeks rather than seconds. Therefore if a particular event is taking place, or unfolding second by second, researchers will be able to obtain more visual information by using Flickr than the standard search engines. An unfortunate but illustrative example here is the terrorist attack on London on 7 July 2005. Within a few minutes of the bombings ordinary people were posting images they had taken onto Flickr, and pools of photographs were created for them to add their images to. No longer were researchers limited to half a dozen photographs that were made available by international media – they could sift through hundreds of photographs that focused on many different aspects of the atrocity.

As a result of the personal nature of Flickr the problem of tagging always arises: and there are many ways in which an event could be described and tagged – to return to the previous example, *London, city, bombing, bombs, terrorist, terrorism, murder, death, attacks, attack, Britain, bus, underground* and so on are some that immediately spring to mind. While this is a legitimate concern and criticism, most searchers are capable of trying a variety of different terms to find appropriate images, or, if all else fails, they can use the option of browsing through a directory structure of subjects to find groups that deal with their subject of interest.

RSS

The speed and functionality of the service can be seen in another useful piece of functionality - that of the RSS feed. Flickr has made feeds available in a variety of different ways, so users can keep up to date with an individual user's collection, being informed almost immediately of any new photographs that have been added, feeds for the discussions in each group or the photographs that have been added to a group.

Mapping

Flickr has recently added new functionality by way of a mapping feature. This allows users to 'geotag' their photographs by adding information to the picture or the location where it was taken. The Flickr map at **www.flickr.com/map** allows searchers to use the map to identify locations and images that use a specific tag, so it is a relatively easy task to find photographs with the tag 'castle' in Scotland, or to simply browse Richmond to see what photographs are available. The weakness of this system is of course that it relies on the ability of individual users of the system to both tag their photographs sensibly and to add the correct geotag information. This obviously limits the potential success of a search.

Contacting the photographer

Another advantage of Flickr over more general search engines is users' ability to engage in conversation with one another. Once a photograph has been identified in the particular area that is of interest to you, or that's pointing the way to answering a query that you have been asked, Flickr gives you a direct link to the photographer. By spending a little time looking through several groups and noticing who posts a lot of photographs I think it is a logical assumption that they have an interest in, and knowledge of, the particular subject they are photographing, whether that be images of New York, cemetery symbolism or beetles. You may wish to contact the photographer via the comments field to ask a question about the specific photograph itself, or you may find it more appropriate to send them an e-mail. If you take a few seconds to look at their profile, and see how frequently they visit the website, it should give you some idea when you may be likely to get a reply - although there is little point sending an e-mail to someone who hasn't updated their photographic collection for several months! Another method that can be employed is to post a more general question to the entire group. Each group has by default a discussion page attached to it. This is also a useful way to ask a question and to receive a reply very quickly, and in many ways is replacing the old stalwart, USENET newsgroups. Depending on the way in which the group has been constituted, questions can be very wide-ranging – they do not have to directly relate to photography at all, but may have a much broader base.

How libraries are using Flickr
Tours

So far we have looked at the ways in which Flickr can be used to obtain information on an individual basis. This is of course very useful, but there are plenty of other ways in which libraries can use the resource by publishing their own photographs. One American library has put online a virtual tour (**www.flickr.com/photos/11329886@N00**), from an external view of the library, through the lobby and into the library itself (see case study below). Viewers can see the children's section, newspaper room and reference stacks. There are also quick 'behind the scenes' views of the staff areas and 'The boss's office'. The tour is brief, under 20 photographs in total, but it fulfils a number of functions: it makes people rather more aware of the existence of the library, it clearly illustrates what resources are available, it is a friendly and welcoming approach, with informal commentaries below each photograph, and it shows that the library is keeping up to speed on technical innovations.

The library is small, so a brief tour of this nature is all that's needed to illustrate appropriate points of information about the institution. However, much larger libraries would find this approach to be of considerable benefit. Links to a Flickr collection could be included on the library home page so that visitors could actually take a stroll around the library before they arrived to orientate themselves – particularly valuable in a big public, reference or university library. Without too much work, sets of photographs could be taken to guide users to particular collections, illustrating the quickest route to the humanities section, for example.

Moreover, photographs of individual staff members could be included (and if there are concerns over privacy their photographs could simply be captioned with their job title rather than individual names) to make it even easier for visitors to work out not only how to get to the humanities section, but the staff member to look out for once they get there.

Events

If a library has held an event, utilizing a Flickr account to record it for posterity would be an excellent use of the resource. Indeed, many libraries are already doing exactly that – a quick search for 'library event' returned over 1000 tagged photographs showing such varied photographs as wildlife displays, children's crafting, author readings, award ceremonies, musical events and more. All these photographs show just how vibrant, interesting and varied library life can be. Almost any event could be recorded, be it a training event, course, presentation or book sale.

Local history

Of course, there is no reason to limit a photographic collection to the here and now – some libraries are putting up historical photographs. There is a fascinating set of images from the American Tutt and Coburn Libraries (**www.flickr.com/photos/tuttlibrary/sets/72057594097880019**) spanning the years 1894 to 2006, with floor plans from the 1960s and photographs of the building process. With easy access to scanners it should be possible to discover old photographs, or even out-of-copyright material from newspapers, that could be incorporated into an interesting visual history of a library, its users, staff and community.

The community

Mention here of community offers up other possibilities. A library should (hopefully) be right at the heart of its community, irrespective of whether that community is based on a campus or a high street, or scattered through a rural area (and there's no reason why the mobile library cannot have its own collection of photographs on the Flickr site), and this can also be reflected in a Flickr account. If a library is collaborating with local history groups, photographs from the wider local community could be added as a collection, well known local citizens could be photographed and short interviews included with their photographs. Retired members of staff could be encouraged to relate stories from their working days, illustrated with appropriate photographs.

Publicity

A Flickr account could be used to publicize what the library is doing. With appropriate permission the covers of new books added to the library collections could be included. Photographs taken of posters advertising forthcoming events could go onto the site, with links back to photographs of the same event that took place the previous year. New members of staff could have their photograph taken and put up for people to meet them virtually. Finally, permission could be granted (via Creative Commons) for other people, organizations or the local press to use the images to further publicize events.

Other utilities

A large number of utilities are associated with Flickr. The Flagrant Disregard site at **http://flagrantdisregard.com/flickr** offers (entirely free of charge) many resources to use existing images in new and different ways, without any necessity for technical knowledge. It is possible to take photographs and turn them into motivational posters, magazine covers, CD covers or even trading cards. I am loath to admit this, but one of the most popular (in terms of most viewed) photographs in my own Flickr collection is my 'Librarian Trading Card', which you can see at **www.flickr.com/photos/philbradley/65070116** – I'm not going to inflict it on you here. Not only can these creations be used with the Flickr account, there is no reason why they should not be reproduced in a printed format for use within the library. At this point the possibilities are limited only by the imagination.

Using Flickr – some considerations

It is of course necessary to evaluate the use, potential use and disadvantages of any resource, Web 2.0 or not. Flickr offers both free and professional accounts. A free account is limited to an upload limit of 10 Mb per month (this is not cumulative – the 'counter' is reset to zero at the beginning of each month). In most instances this should not prove to be very much of a barrier since this will allow a user to upload dozens of photographs every month, depending of course on the size of individual pictures. (Almost any graphics package will provide you with multiple ways of shrinking the size of your files to something more manageable.) A slightly more important limitation is that each free account is limited to only three different 'sets' or collections of images. When an image is uploaded users can title the image, add a description and tags, and also decide what group or groups to add the image to. They can also create their own sets of images – think of them as folders. One set may be photographs of the library, another of members of staff – leaving only one other folder available. If the intention is to upload a lot of photographs then consideration should be given to purchasing an annual professional account.

Free accounts do have other limitations: they may be deleted after 90 days of inactivity, individual photographs can be no larger in size than 5 Mb (which should not in most cases be a problem) and up to only 200 photographs (the most recent ones) will be displayed, although more can be stored – they are not automatically deleted. These restrictions are not particularly onerous, however, and should not cause any great difficulties for a library wishing to explore the use of publishing photographs on the service. The cost of a commercial account is (at the time of writing) less than $25/£15 per year, and this allows users to have an unlimited number of sets of photographs and an upload limit of 2 Gb.

Unfortunately it is also necessary to add that Flickr has come under criticism in the past for allowing adult images to be hosted on its servers, and some (American) libraries have received anonymous e-mails suggesting that they should limit or indeed cease their involvement with the service. This is discussed in some detail in the Flickr group Libraries and Librarians at **www.flickr.com/groups/librariesandlibrarians**, and the general consensus is that there is little, if anything, to be concerned about. While it is true that adult images are available on the system, Flickr does police photographs very closely, and anything that may be objectionable can be flagged by any user. Images of an adult nature are tagged as private and shared with friends only, and it is necessary to specifically hunt out this type of material.

On a less controversial note, there are a number of groups that will be of interest to librarians, including, as well as the previously mentioned Libraries and Librarians, Librarians in Glasses at **www.flickr.com/groups/ 59742117@N00**, and Librarian Trading Cards at **www.flickr.com/groups/ librariancards**. There is also a group to allow people to share photographs they have taken of the Nancy Pearl librarian action figure at **www.flickr.com/groups/nancypearl**. A quick search for 'librarians' in the group search function returned over 80 different groups and over ten times that number when searching for 'libraries'.

Using Flickr – the practicalities

Flickr is a relatively simple application to use – the most difficult part of the whole process is getting registered in the first instance. As Flickr is owned by Yahoo! it is necessary to create a Yahoo! account first or, if you already have one, you can obviously circumnavigate that section. Simply follow the necessary link to the Yahoo! sign-up page and input the required details to register with the system. You can then sign into your Flickr account.

Figure 10.1
The Flickr menu

Perhaps the first thing to do if you're a photographer is to upload some photographs you wish to share. Try to keep the file size reasonable, or it will take a long time to upload, and will quickly eat into your monthly allowance. A good picture size to start with is 800 x 600 pixels. Under the Flickr logo in the top left-hand corner is a menu bar. Click on the down triangle next to the 'You' option, as shown in Figure 10.1

Clicking on 'Upload Photos' opens a second dialogue box, as seen in Figure 10.2. This dialogue box will keep you informed as to the amount of bandwidth you have left in any given month, and once it reaches 100% you'll need to be patient and wait for the first of the month to roll around again. Unfortunately you cannot just delete any images that you've already uploaded to made room, since the restriction is on the amount of data that you've transferred, not how much file space you've

Upload photos to Flickr

You have used

0%

of your upload capacity for this month.

(You have a limit of 2 GB per month.)

Your upload limit is measured in bandwidth, or "throughput", **not** actual storage space. More information...

Uploading tools

We provide tools for Mac and Windows to make it easy to upload a batch of photos all at once.

Find the image(s) you want on your computer

1. [   ] Browse...
2. [   ] Browse...
3. [   ] Browse...
4. [   ] Browse...
5. [   ] Browse...
6. [   ] Browse...

Add tags for ALL these images [?]

[   ]

Choose the privacy settings [?]

○ Private
  ☐ Visible to Friends
  ☐ Visible to Family
◉ Public

Reproduced with permission of Yahoo! Inc. © 2007 by Yahoo! Inc. FLICKR and the FLICKR logo are trademarks of Yahoo! Inc.

Figure 10.2
The Flickr 'Upload photos' dialogue box

used up. Until then, however, simply find the image or images on your computer that you want to upload. You can then add tags to the image(s). The tags are your own words to describe important aspects or points about the photographs. Flickr does not use any controlled vocabulary or thesaurus, and prefers to leave it up to individual users to decide what is appropriate themselves. Of course, it's not compulsory to add any tags at all, but that would make it very much more difficult for users to search for and find your images. Some photographs are tagged with only one or two, while others use dozens; it's an entirely personal choice.

Once a photograph has been uploaded you can retitle it and add a description to provide more information about the image if appropriate. Flickr provides another resource that can be downloaded to make the process of uploading images slightly easier – available from the Tools section of the site at **www.flickr.com/tools**. Photographs can then be added to sets that individual users create. This is very straightforward, as can be seen in Figure 10.3 (overleaf).

My wife and I had been driving along the motorway and we saw a play cottage being towed along and took a photograph of it. This is not the type of image that we usually take, so I added a new set to my Flickr collection along the lines of 'Well I never!'. This was a useful first step to take, but only people who know me would see the photograph, and photographers, like writers, want their work to be seen by as many people as possible. I felt sure that there must be groups on Flickr where people post similar strange photographs. Clicking on the 'Groups' menu option allowed me to run a search for appropriate groups, and in this instance I thought that a search for 'strange' was appropriate. As you can see from Figure 10.4 (overleaf), there were over

Figure 10.3 Tagging an uploaded
photograph using Flickr

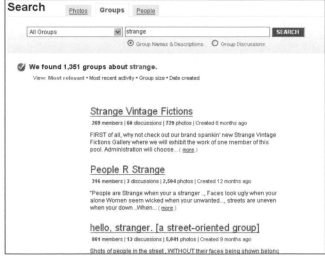

Figure 10.4 Flickr groups related to the term 'strange'

1300 groups that had some sort of relationship to the word strange. Flickr
displays results in relevance-ranked order, but has several ways of re-ranking
results, by time frame, group activity or size for example. One group seemed

to be appropriate – 'Strange things', described as 'Anything strange, odd, surreal, absurd, unusual, abnormal, out-of-place, out-of-ordinary'. Once I'd joined this group I was then able to add the image I'd taken. Until and unless I choose to remove it from that group any other members of that group will be able to see the image I'm sharing, unless the owner or moderator deletes it.

Clearly there is a great deal more than can be done with Flickr, but this section provides some of the basics, while at the same time illustrating that it is easy to join, simple to add photographs and straightforward to share them. Any library could set up a free account and start posting photographs literally within a few minutes, without any technical knowledge. It takes little more work to start your own group on Flickr as well, which can be administered by a member of staff, and the photographs in the group made public, private or access-limited to certain named individuals.

Case study: A library using Flickr

The Johnson County Library in Kansas has its own website at **www. jocolibrary.org**, but it has also created a Flickr tour of one of the branch libraries, Lackman, at **http://flickr.com/photos/11329886@N00**. Scott Sime, who is an information specialist at Lackman, explained in some detail why the library chose to create a tour using Flickr.

Q: Can you tell me a little bit about the library to put it into some sort of perspective and context for me?
A: Our library system [consists] of 12 branch locations and one larger main library. We currently have almost 400 employees (379, as of last year). The system serves about 400,000 people.
Q: What gave you the idea of creating a library tour in photographic format?
A: I attended a workshop for Technology in Kansas Libraries, and one of the sessions was how to use Flickr, presented by Joshua Neff of Olathe Public Library and Mickey Coalwell with the Northeast Kansas Library Association (NEKLS). They showed us a lot of great things you can do with Flickr.

Q: Why did you decide to use Flickr?

A: I use Flickr for sharing some of my personal photos, and it was natural for me to turn to it again for this. Flickr makes uploading, organizing and tagging photos very easy. Our library has also started using Flickr for other projects, and we've since developed a set of guidelines including generic tags to use for each photo, making them easier to find.

Q: Did you consider using any of the other photograph-sharing resources out there?

A: I was aware of others, like Photobucket at **www.photobucket.com** or ImageShack at **http://imageshack.us**, but it was my personal experience with Flickr that made me go with it. Ease of use was a big consideration.

Q: Who suggested putting the tour online? Was it necessary to go through any 'hoops' to do it, or was it just a case of 'great . . . go for it!'?

A: The idea originally was from Joshua Neff and Mickey Coalwell, but I adapted it to work with our library. There were minimal hoops to jump through. My supervisor was enthusiastic and supportive, and our web team was great as well. Since we've put this online, we have developed some guidelines for using these cool new 2.0 tools (like standardized image tags), so there are a few more hoops now, but they're relatively painless.

Q: You've not really included any photographs that depict identifiable individuals, such as patrons or staff – was there a particular reason for that?

A: My first priority for the tour was to showcase the physical location. This virtual tour is the first step in what I hope to be a regularly updated Flickr account.

Also, to include patrons in photos, the patrons must sign a photo-release waiver before we can post their pictures online, so posting photos of patrons can be a little trickier.

Q: Why did you include the photographs you chose? What 'feeling' (if any) were you hoping to get across with your choices? In other words, what message should the library tour be giving people?

A: I wanted to give people an overview of both what our library looks like to patrons, but also what goes on behind the scenes. The first contact that some of our patrons may have with our library is online. Now they can come in with an idea of what our library looks like and how it's laid out.

Q: Have you publicized your Flickr tour/account to anyone in other library literature, or are you thinking of doing so?

A: We link to our Flickr tour on our website **www.jocolibrary.org** and also publicize the online tour in the library blogosphere.

Q: Is this something you're considering expanding? If so, are there any specific things that you think you'll add to the Flickr collection, such as staff, photographs of events, etc.?

A: I would like to see each of our branches have a tour like this. We are already putting some other photosets online, like book/topic displays and library programmes. Of course, we also have lots of photos of patrons and library events on the library's website.

Q: Tags: did you spend any time over the tags that you used, or just use tags that seemed immediately obvious? Are you thinking of adding the photographs to any of the library/librarian-orientated groups on Flickr?

A: When I first put the tour up, I used tags that seemed obvious: Library, JCL, etc. But we've worked with our web team to define what tags we will use on future projects. We want to ensure that all Johnson County Library photos available in Flickr are joined together via tags – regardless of which branch posted the photos.

Q: Have you had any feedback yet on what you've done?

A: I've only had feedback from staff, but it's been positive so far!

Other photograph-sharing resources

As previously mentioned, Flickr is not the only utility that offers people the ability to share their photographs with each other, and indeed it is not an exaggeration to say that this is probably the single most popular Web 2.0 growth area, with the possible exception of social bookmarking. In fact, according to a Hitwise report in June 2006 (**http://weblogs.hitwise. com/leeann-prescott/2006/06/photobucket_leads_photo_ sharin.html**) Flickr was only ranked at no. 6 in the popularity stakes.

Photobucket

Photobucket at **www.photobucket.com** provides free photograph-sharing facilities, as well as video sharing. In common with many other applications it also has a professional version with increased storage, bandwidth, premium support and no advertising. The emphasis of Photobucket is, however, slightly different from that of Flickr. Enhancements to Flickr emphasize the social nature of sharing photographs with friends, colleagues and strangers. Photobucket, on the other hand, has as its particular strength the ability to store images and make them readily available for use by other resources. For example, a lot of the usage of Photobucket (according to Hitwise, 56%) is from users of the MySpace system. When a user adds a photograph to the Photobucket system the image cannot be tagged or added to a group in the way that is offered by Flickr. Users are limited to adding the image to specific sub-folders that they create (similar to Flickr sets) and adding their own description.

The power of Photobucket, however, lies in the fact that each photograph has three different links: a URL link (for e-mail and IM), an HTML tag (for websites and blogs) and IMG code (for forums and bulletin boards). Consequently, if users wish to include a link to an image in a bulletin board posting they are writing, in a weblog or in some other social system it is very simple and straightforward to do so. While it's possible to add a Flickr image to a weblog it is slightly tricky, and it is more difficult again to incorporate images stored on Flickr to other resources. While Photobucket has limited functionality, therefore, its attraction lies in its flexibility and ease of use.

Kodak Gallery

The Kodak Gallery at **www.kodakgallery.com** offers users the ability to upload photographs, share them with friends, and view and edit photographs. As may be expected from the name, the site is run by the Kodak group and consequently has a largely commercial aspect to it; users can purchase hard-copy prints and create tailored merchandise with images on, such as tote bags, coasters, calendars, mugs, photobooks and so on. Obviously this resource is visiting the whole question of photograph-sharing from an entirely different angle, but the ability to purchase products may be of some interest to libraries. Many public libraries do now sell different items to their users, from used books and DVDs upwards. A little creative thought could go into creating a library calendar for the year (with associated details about opening hours and so on), or mugs with the library logo on them or even mouse mats and puzzles with appropriate images on them. Items do not need to be ordered in bulk and can be purchased individually, so this may be an excellent way of publicizing an event or competition, for example, with the winner receiving a mug with their photograph and the library logo on it.

Zoto

Zoto at **www.zoto.com** promises to let you 'do more with your digital photos'. There are the usual free and professional accounts available to users of the system, with paying users able to utilize photographs with their weblogs, for example. Users can store, tag and share images. One interesting feature of Zoto is the ability to create galleries that are open to other people to contribute their own photographs of an event – useful if you want to encourage a local community of users to increase their involvement by acting almost like photographic journalists at the events you are holding. While it is true that this can be done using Flickr, Zoto has in large part simplified the process and made it rather more 'personal'. It has a well-developed interface, which is straightforward and easy to use. However, the search functionality is not as developed as the Flickr offering, and it is somewhat slow.

Zooomr

Zooomr at **http://beta.zooomr.com/home** has received a lot of good press since its arrival. It has an interesting concept and idea as to what a photograph is – rather than something which is a static object in and of itself, it is viewed as the basis for a story. Users can geotag images (which is something that Flickr has just added, but with a slightly less smooth interface) to indicate to other people exactly where an image was taken. It is also possible to see photographs that were taken nearby, which puts the original photograph into a better context. Sound can be added to images as well.

The possibilities for use within a library environment are varied. It is easy to create a library tour, with embedded commentary at various points. Not only can the library be the focus for a tour, but an entire university campus could be covered in a similar manner, with students adding their own images of buildings and so on. School pupils could collaborate on a local history project with a teacher or librarian, and events, meetings or talks could also be captured.

Other resources

The list of photograph-sharing resources is long, and those discussed above are simply a selection of those available. Readers may wish to check out some of the others before deciding which one to use:

- BubbleShare at **www.bubbleshare.com**
- Fotopic at **www.fotopic.net**
- Funtigo at **www.funtigo.com**
- Hello at **www.hello.com**
- My Photo Album at **www.myphotoalbum.com**
- Pbase at **www.pbase.com**
- Photosite at **www.photosite.com**
- Picasa at **http://picasa.google.com**
- PictureTrail at **www.picturetrail.com**
- Shutterfly at **www.shutterfly.com**
- SmugMug at **www.smugmug.com**
- Snapfish at **http://www1.snapfish.co.uk**

- Webshots at **www.webshots.com**
- 23HQ at **www.23hq.com**
- 43 Places at **www.43places.com**

Conclusion

In the early years of the internet information was available only as text and it really wasn't until the advent of the world wide web that images were able to come into their own. However, an image isn't just a picture, of course – it's a repository of considerable information in its own right. The use of Web 2.0 resources to publish images, to tag and share the content contained in them, and to then use that as the basis for building a community or enhancing an existing one, is both powerful and exciting. Libraries can create their own photographic content, encourage their users to do the same and produce information in entirely different ways, that even a few years ago would have been unthinkable.

URLs mentioned in this chapter

www.23hq.com
www.43places.com
http://beta.zooomr.com/home
www.bubbleshare.com
http://flagrantdisregard.com/flickr
www.flickr.com
www.flickr.com/creativecommons
www.flickr.com/groups/59742117@N00
www.flickr.com/groups/librariancards
www.flickr.com/groups/librariesandlibrarians
www.flickr.com/groups/nancypearl
www.flickr.com/map
www.flickr.com/photos/11329886@N00
www.flickr.com/photos/tuttlibrary/sets/72057594097880019
www.flickr.com/search
www.flickr.com/search/advanced
www.flickr.com/tools
www.fotopic.net

www.funtigo.com
www.hello.com
http://imageshack.us
www.jocolibrary.org
www.kodakgallery.com
www.myphotoalbum.com
www.pbase.com
www.photobucket.com
www.photosite.com
http://picasa.google.com
www.picturetrail.com
www.shutterfly.com
www.smugmug.com
http://weblogs.hitwise.com/leeann-prescott/2006/06/photobucket_
    leads_photo_sharin.html
www.webshots.com
http://www1.snapfish.co.uk
www.zoto.com

Chapter 11

Miscellaneous resources

Introduction

One of the major difficulties with a subject such as Web 2.0 is the sheer volume of resources being created – either by individuals in their garages at the weekend, for fun as much as anything else, or by organizations, both large and small, that are hoping to sell their product to one of the major players for millions of dollars. I am informed of new products on a daily basis, and if I were to sit and try them all out I would never get any work done!

However, I would like to at least mention as many of them as I can, with if possible a little explanation and some ideas as to how you might find them useful. I do this in the knowledge that you'll almost certainly look at a lot of them, scratch your head and move on to one of the others, which you will find useful. But I hope at least a few readers will find every one of the following resources to be useful enough to explore in more detail and perhaps incorporate in their work. It's also worth pointing out that not all of these will fall fairly and squarely under the Web 2.0 banner, but this is less of a concern, since I'm taking a fairly pragmatic viewpoint as to what resources are or are not Web 2.0 based. My major questions when looking at each of the resources were 'Does it work as expected?' and 'Is it useful within a library or information centre environment in some way?' If the answer in both cases is 'yes', then I considered it for inclusion.

Collaboration services

We have established that one of the main focal points of Web 2.0 resources is the ability to share knowledge, experience, thoughts, ideas and opinions within specific groups or within a wider context with anyone who is interested. Almost any of the utilities mentioned in previous chapters could be included here, and it would not have taken a great deal of work to put any of the following in their place; there is never just one way of doing something.

Obviously tools already exist to allow people to collaborate; pen, paper and a cork board are between them a fairly useful resource. However, when we're dealing with colleagues who may be geographically spread across a wide area, or indeed inhabiting different time zones, it does help to have resources that can be shared by everyone. It's a lot easier to have a document in one place, for example, and to allow everyone access to it rather than take copies, send them out to a dozen people, get them all back with comments and alterations, and try to make sense of the patchwork quilt you are left with.

Sharing desktops

Sharing start pages with a resource such as Pageflakes, mentioned in Chapter 5, is one way of sharing a desktop, in that everyone has access to the same links and resources. However, this can be extended further. Central Desktop at **www.centraldesktop.com** allows an entire team to work together on project tracking, task management, shared calendars and so on. Joyent at **www.joyent.com** works in a similar fashion, with e-mail, calendars, contacts databases and other shared applications. Since these are aimed at a commercial market they are priced products. Other applications you might want to explore are Near-Time at **www.near-time.net** and MyWebDesktop at **www.mywebdesktop.net**.

Office-based tools

Word processors, spreadsheet packages, presentation software and so on are no longer entirely within the realm of Microsoft (if indeed they ever were). Many different packages exist to allow users to share data back and forth. Good examples are the Google Docs & Spreadsheets resource at **http://docs.google.com** and SlideShare at **www.slideshare.net** (see p. 47).

The Google resource looks very much like a straightforward Microsoft Windows product, and if you can use a word processor or spreadsheet package you won't have any problem working out how to use it. What makes the product different is the opportunity to allow other people to directly collaborate and assist with editing a document, or just viewing it. Google also allows users to publish the document, either to a URL that it provides, or to a weblog.

However, we need not stop with just those. Cl1p, at **http://cl1p.net**, is self-styled as 'The internet clip board'. It is designed to allow users to quickly cut and paste text to a web page that they create, and which can be visited by other people to view, share and copy the content. It's a quick and easy way of sharing content, but it can also be used to create a notebook, a basic personalized forum between friends or colleagues (pages can be passworded for added privacy), and various Cl1p resources can be linked together.

Users of gOffice at **www.goffice.com** can create word-processed documents, spreadsheets, presentations and so on, with the added benefit that these can be turned into Adobe Acrobat PDF files. Dabble at **www.dabbledb.com** is a similar product in that it also allows users to create documents, group spreadsheets and customized databases, and it focuses on a corporate approach. 'The best online office on Earth' is how ThinkFree at **www.thinkfree.com** describes itself. The resources are compatible with Microsoft Office and include all of the functionality you would expect, and it's also platform independent, so it will work in a Windows, Apple or Linux environment. The Zoho Virtual Office at **www.zoho.com/ virtual-office** includes opportunities for using webmail, calendars, writing and sharing documents, tasks, reports, contacts, notes, instant messaging and so on. It is free for individual use and there is a corporate version available for organizations.

Once again I think it's worth pointing out that this is just a very small subset of the utilities and resources that are available – hundreds more exist, but this is a representative collection of them.

E-mail services

We all have e-mail, and there isn't anything particularly new or exciting about it, of course. While most of us feel we can't live without it, there are times when it can be a source of irritation, especially when we get unwanted commercial e-mail, and fear of an increase in junk mail can make us less likely to provide personal details. However, there are a number of resources that simplify the whole issue, and these are throw-away accounts which can be used a number of times, or for a specific period of time, and then they just disappear into the ether. Consequently they can be a really useful way of signing up for a service that requires a confirmation e-mail address, or in situations when you're not entirely sure that you won't be put onto commercial mailing lists. Several of them will also provide an RSS feed, so you do not have to keep visiting the site to check whether any mail has arrived. The vast majority of these services are entirely free, and the creator makes a small amount of money (usually) by hosting advertisements supplied by Google on the site. As one of the terms and conditions imposed by Google, the site owners are not allowed to encourage users to click on adverts, but I'd like to suggest that if the service provided suits you, take a moment every now and then to click on an advert for a product or site that interests you; it really does make a difference to the owner of a site in that over a period of time they can earn enough money to help pay for the upkeep of their site.

A good resource to try in this category is TempInbox at **www.tempinbox. com/English**, which allows users to create an address ending in @tempinbox.com without even visiting the site first. When you wish to check e-mail, simply visit the site, input the address and view and delete any e-mail as appropriate. Obviously most general names have already been used (simply type in your own first name, for example – someone has almost certainly set up a box for it already), but to an extent that doesn't matter, because you can't send e-mail from it, just receive. However, since anyone can look at the content of any e-mail address it would be unwise to have sensitive material sent to a common named account, so create something that is unusual and unlikely to be used by other people. When you do not need the account any longer, simply forget it and walk away.

Alternatively, try SpamBob at **http://spambob.com**, which comes in three variants: an e-mail account that can be checked at the SpamBob site, an address that forwards e-mail to your 'real' account and which can be disabled at any time, and a third account where mail is simply deleted, for those times that you just have to provide a valid e-mail address. Mailnull at **http://mailnull.com** provides similar functionality by allowing you to create multiple addresses which then re-route e-mails to your proper account.

Other services worth looking at are:

- 10 Minute Mail at **http://10minutemail.com/10MinuteMail/index. html**
- Dodgeit at **http://dodgeit.com**
- Mailinator at **www.mailinator.com/mailinator/index.jsp**
- PookMail at **www.pookmail.com/about.php**
- Spamgourmet at **www.spamgourmet.com**
- Spamhole at **www.spamhole.com/create.html**
- Sneakemail at **http://sneakemail.com**

The MailChimp service at **www.mailchimp.com**, allows you to quickly and easily set up a mailing service for newsletters or subscriber opt-in lists. Users purchase 'stamps' which can then be used to send out e-mails using the service. FutureMe at **http://futureme.org** allows you to send yourself an e-mail, to the address and date specified. It could be used as a memory aid, for example. It's proved very popular, with over 350,000 e-mails sent into the future.

Poster, banner and picture creation

The phrase 'a picture is worth 1000 words' is as true now as it has ever been. Unfortunately for most of us, we're not particularly good at graphic design, photography or drawing; I know from bitter experience that trying to produce a banner from scratch almost always leads to total failure. However, there are a lot of services available that can be used to create banners and posters which not only have the advantage of looking very professional, but can be memorable, raise a smile and require no artistic ability from you. If you need to create an eye-catching display within your library or information centre and are stuck for ideas, then some of the resources coming up may be exactly what you need, and even if you don't use them directly they'll certainly give you some inspiration.

Some ideas that may appeal are:

- posters drawing attention to different services the library offers
- greeting cards for new members of staff, patrons or course delegates
- weblog images
- avatars for your forums, profiles, blogs, etc. (an avatar is a graphic representation of a person, either accurate or perhaps in cartoon form)
- button images (both on-screen buttons and pin-on badges)
- address labels
- name tags
- place tags
- RSS buttons for your site or weblog
- comic strips (a great example being at **www.libraryforlife.org/blogs/ lifeline/?p=2504**)
- reminder/post-it notes
- web award generators.

If some of these can be incorporated into events or work you are doing with colleagues they can become talking points that help promote not only the specific service or function, but the information centre as well.

The Custom Sign Generator at **www.customsigngenerator.com** offers thousands of pre-generated images which simply require you to plug in the text that you want displayed. There are photographs, logos, parody pictures, support ribbons, silly book covers and so on.

The Tombstone Generator at **www.jjchandler.com/tombstone** creates a tombstone with whatever text you want placed on it. Although this sounds rather morbid it was the perfect resource to provide me with an opening image for a talk I was giving on 'The death of search' at a conference.

The Yahoo!-style Logo Maker at **http://logo54.com/net/yahoo** is a fun resource that lets you input text which is then rendered in a very recognizable font indeed. This could be used on a web page or printed out and used in any manner of different ways. Figure 11.1 shows an example, though to appreciate it fully you'll need to think of it in bright red!

ENQUIRY DESK

Reproduced by permission of Yahoo! Inc. © 2007 by Yahoo! Inc. YAHOO! and the YAHOO! logo are trademarks of Yahoo! Inc.

Figure 11.1 A Yahoo!-like sign

The same thing can be done with Google, as Figure 11.2 demonstrates, though once again colour is needed to provide the full impact. This resource is at the Google Logo Maker at **www. littlefunny.com/Google.aspx**.

Librarians are great!

Reproduced with thanks.

Figure 11.2 Creating a heading using a Google-like font

The advantage of this particular service is that it also creates a search page with a URL that could be used to search Google, and you can see this in operation at **www.littlefunny.com/ShowGoogle.aspx?logo=Librarians %20are%20great!**. While I wouldn't suggest using this for anything serious there are times when it might be appropriate.

Another image generator, with the advantage of having a professional twist to it, is the library catalogue-card generator at **www.blyberg.net/card-generator**: an example is shown in Figure 11.3 (overleaf).

Storage and transmission services

Improving technology is wonderful, but does bring with it completely new problems, and one of these is the creation of really large files. Even the simplest document, spreadsheet or presentation seems to balloon in size, and it can make them very difficult to send as attachments; your e-mail system may simply refuse to handle a file over a certain size, and there

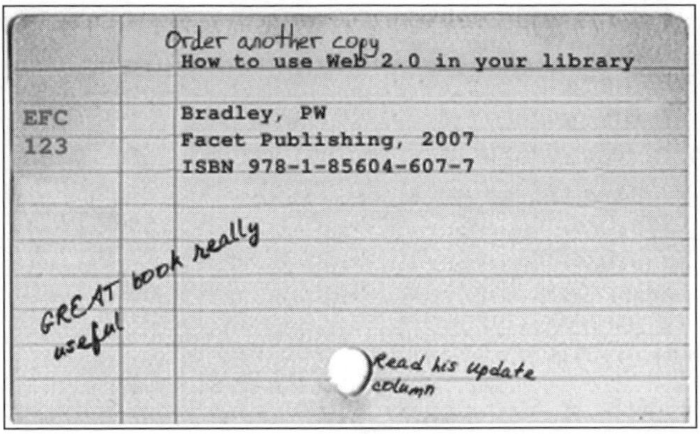

With thanks to John Blyberg for his permission to use this screen-shot.

Figure 11.3 Catalogue-card generator image

is no guarantee that your recipient's system will be any better. However, there are a number of utilities that can be used to either store large files, or that can be used as an intermediate system to make the whole process much less painful.

YouSendIt at **www.yousendit.com** allows you to upload a file or number of files up to 100 Mb in size (or 2 Gb for a commercial version) which can then be picked up by the recipient using their browser to download the file, rather than e-mail. 30gigs at **www.30gigs.com** is a service that provides its users with (yes, you guessed it) 30 gigabytes of storage space, while Box at **www.box.net** offers 1 Gb of space for free and a resource or utility to allow you to provide a link to files via your website or weblog. Meanwhile, Multiply at **http://multiply.com** provides unlimited storage space for a weblog, photographs, video and so on. These can also be shared and your content can be used as the basis for discussions.

Discovery services

The bane of every public librarian's life must surely be the question 'This was really good. Do you have anything else like it?', while someone waves a paperback at them from the latest blockbusting author. Fortunately there are now various guidance services that users can be pointed towards, or which could be used as the basis of an event, discussion group or promotion. Many of the resources work not just with the latest paperbacks, but with non-fiction material as well, though admittedly with perhaps slightly less success. These services are not entirely new – the online bookstore Amazon at **www.amazon.co.uk** has been working with this concept for several years now: if you are registered with Amazon you will be quite familiar with its lists of suggestions, based upon your previous purchases.

Books

A very quick and simple resource to use is Literature-Map at **http://literature-map.com**, which merely requires the name of an author. It will then create a map for you, based around that author – the closer to your choice another author is on the screen, the more similar they are. Figure 11.4 displays a map based on Charles Darwin.

Reproduced with thanks.

Figure 11.4
A literature map of Charles Darwin

ConnectViaBooks at **www.connectviabooks.com** works on a slightly different principle, in that you are instructed to input either a book title or an author to start the system. You are then presented with a list of titles and will be offered similar works, together with a list of users who have expressed a preference for the same author or title. There may also be discussion topics available for you to take part in. What Should I Read Next? at **www.whatshouldireadnext.com** has a database of over 20,000 books and will suggest a title based on something you have previously read. DebbiesIdea at **www.debbiesidea.com** takes a slightly different twist to the concept: users suggest what book to read first for an unfamiliar author. Lib.rario.us at **http://lib.rario.us** is a site that is used to tag and catalogue collections of books, music or movies.

Perhaps the best known of all of these services is the LibraryThing resource at **www.librarything.com**, which currently has catalogued over 8 million books. The service is designed for users to catalogue their own book collections, tag the books, share them with other people, get involved with discussion groups, review books and so on. Importantly, the service can be used in conjunction with weblogs and search, allowing people to search through your collection. As you might expect, the library community has championed LibraryThing, and there is a discussion group specifically of/for librarians who use the service at **www.librarything.com/groups/ librarianswholibrar** (that abruptly truncated URL is actually correct; it's not a typographical error), so it may be worth making that an early stop on any tour of the system. It is free for a limited number of books, and there is a payment option for unlimited use.

Music

Similar resources are available for those with a more musical bent. Music-Map at **www.music-map.com** is based on the same concept as Literature-Map. Pandora at **www. pandora.com** is designed as a personalized radio station, with users 'teaching' the system by rating each song as it is played, and over the course of time the playlist becomes more attuned to that individual's listening preferences. Indy at **http://indy.tv** is a software download that focuses on independent music. If that doesn't interest you, it's worth trying Liveplasma at **www.liveplasma.com** or Last.fm at **www.last.fm**, which dubs itself 'The social music revolution'.

Movies

MyFilmz at **http://myfilmz.net** has listed over 20,000 films and, as you would expect, is designed to let users add their favourite films, and review, tag and discuss them with other people who share similar interests. Ajaxilicious at **http://movies.ajaxilicious.be** is an online movie database/catalogue of your films which can be shared with others via RSS or the Ajaxilicious interface. Another possibility is the Movielens site at **http://movielens.umn.edu/login** provided by the University of Minnesota.

Other discovery utilities

While books, music and movies are the three areas that have been concentrated on, they are by no means the only ones. Dine52 at **www.dine52.com** is a shared recipe site, Mightyv at **www.mightyv.com** helps viewers in the UK find new television programmes to watch, while

TV.com at **www.tv.com** and TitanTV at **http://ww1.titantv.com** do the same for an American audience.

Using discovery services within a library environment

Most of the services mentioned above are based completely in popular culture, and while they may sometimes be useful within a commercial, corporate environment, I think that will be the exception rather than the rule. For other types of information and library service, however, the possibilities are wide-ranging. Within a public library, users who ask the 'What shall I read/watch/listen to next?' question can be guided to an appropriate resource. If an event is being planned, based on a particular author, band, genre or film, then the librarian who is short of time could plug one or two suggestions into the resources and see what comes out, and the basics of a display or presentation are soon created.

A community group (be it students, children, public library users) could be created, and the suggestions from one of the discovery resources would be a great way of providing a starting point for a discussion. Furthermore, if everyone in the community joined the same resource they could use a tag to identify themselves as members of that community: this would be an excellent way for everyone to get to know each other, and new members could break the ice by spending some time taking a look at other members' collections and interests.

Those resources that include RSS feeds could supplement a weblog, portal or website. Incorporating feeds into other Web 2.0 resources and pointing the group towards them would be a quick, easy and effective way to keep a group together and involved. Of course, there is no reason why you should have to think in terms of a community as being based on a group of individuals who all share a similar geographic space - if you are a school librarian it could be an interesting challenge to work with a colleague from another school to create a shared book club, perhaps. Public librarians could work with their counterparts in any towns or cities that their own community has twinned with in other countries. A portal based on a book club that in turn draws content from the tagged and shared books of its users could be a fascinating experiment - and experience!

Social networking

The previous section should have provided some food for thought on different ways in which Web 2.0 resources can be used. Some of the tools that we have looked at earlier in the book, such as Zimbio or wikis, do allow groups to work together, but it is worth pointing out that there are social networking services that have been specifically created to draw groups of people together to share knowledge, interests and experiences. Some of these are in fact right in the vanguard of Web 2.0, and readers who have teenage sons or daughters will already be aware of MySpace at **www.myspace.com** which has proved to be a huge success, although in the UK British teenagers often prefer Bebo, which you can find at **www.bebo.com**. Users are able to create their own profiles and share photographs, videos, journals and so on, create their own networks of friends and meet new people who share similar interests.

Librarians need to be aware of what teenagers are doing within spaces such as this, particularly if they are public, school or academic librarians, with young people as a core client group. An understanding of these resources, even if they are not currently being used, is necessary in order to keep in touch with and have an understanding of this group. Failure in this regard may increasingly lead to the library being sidelined, while a deeper understanding of, and contact and discussion with, students within this arena can have exactly the opposite effect. Although MySpace is widely used by teenagers, it is only one example of social networking, and there are plenty of others.

Blogtronix at **www.blogtronix.com** is aimed at corporate users who want to integrate weblogs, wikis, podcasting, documents, RSS feeds – in fact anything that can be created and shared. CollectiveX at **www. collectivex.com** is a private and secure network including a group calendar, discussions, file sharing, social networking, profiling and so on. TagWorld at **www.tagworld.com**, Towncrossing at **www.towncrossing. com**, LinkedIn at **www.linkedin.com** and Meetup at **www.meetup.com** are other examples of this type of resource. Some of them are commercial in nature, and others are free, so it is worth looking at several of them to decide if they are going to be of use.

Social networks are of course useful for lots of different types of groups, many of which could benefit from the involvement of a local library or information centre:

■ Private clubs, such as book review clubs, could easily share information back and forth, with discussions on various book-related topics, information on the next meeting or individual input into a shared weblog on books members have read recently.
■ A business chamber needs to keep its members involved and interested, so the involvement of a local library that could provide details of new resources of interest to the group would clearly be beneficial.
■ A departmental grouping may wish to discuss and share information that is of interest only to that specific group, rather than everyone in the organization. A network of this nature would be helped with social networking software, especially if the group is scattered geographically. The information staff would still be able to provide useful information and resources, however, no matter how widely spread the group members are.
■ Residential associations need to keep up to date with what is happening in their area, and a public library, acting as a central resource for local information, could keep a high profile by providing appropriate information and plugging it into the network.

Membership groups, associations, clubs, faith-based groups, families, political groups, schools and alumni associations, and boards can all make use of social networking resources.

Mashups

No book on any aspect of the internet published this year would be complete without some reference to 'mashups'. A mashup is a resource created out of two or more others – for example, creating a photographic map of a country or region by combining images from Flickr with the Google Maps system. Some of these can be very useful as information resources in their own right, or in combination with yet other tools.

Bitty Browser

The Bitty Browser at **www.bitty.com** is a small utility used on a web page or in a weblog which acts as a small browser, allowing someone to visit another page while remaining on the original site. You can also get the Bitty Browser to automatically load content for you, such as a Google search, or a link into a news website, and so on. If you can imagine one of those situations in the movies when the bad guy, intent on world destruction, is keeping up to date with the news by looking at dozens of television screens at once, you have the right idea – just think of numerous Bitty Browsers instead of television screens and you have it.

ChaCha

ChaCha at **www.chacha.com** is a search system that routes your enquiry to a real human being or 'guide' who can work with you in order to get the best answer to your question. This is very similar to an 'ask a librarian' system, and users rate guides on their helpfulness and so on. Searches are kept available and matched against new queries, with the hope of creating a better set of results every time. By combining chat with search users hopefully get exactly what they need. A system like this may be useful in a situation where the library or information service offers a chat option, but is unable to provide as much coverage as it would like.

Supreme Court Zeitgeist

The Supreme Court Zeitgeist at **http://judgejohnroberts.com** is a site that offers information on the US Supreme Court by combining elements from Google News, del.icio.us, Technorati and Amazon.

Liveplasma

Liveplasma at **http://liveplasma.com** combines music, mapping and information from the Amazon bookseller that shows interrelationships between albums, artists, movies and so on to reveal interesting connections between groups or individuals, and which could easily be used in conjunction with one of the discovery services mentioned earlier.

Mashups are a hugely popular area. Some work better than others, but what may have little to offer one person can be an excellent concept for someone else, so they're always worth looking at, just in case you find a gem. If you have five minutes to spare, try some of these:

- AllYourWords at **http://allyourwords.com** associates specific words with specific websites – a little like the Google 'lucky' button
- Daily Mashup at **http://dailymashup.com** provides links to the day's popular news stories, images and links
- Doggdot at **http://doggdot.us** is a combination of del.icio.us, Slashdot and Digg – all sites that offer bookmarking.

Mapping services

Very closely allied to mashups are sites that allow users to create their own maps, and in fact it would have been perfectly possible to include the following resources in the previous category, except that there are so many of them.

Maps and local mapping services are not an innovation on the net – they have been around for a long time, and all the major search engines provide excellent local map functionality by allowing users to search by postal or zip code, to search for hotels in a particular location, to view satellite maps or to get a set of directions from A to B. Useful as this may be, there is little that users can do actively with these resources themselves, other than perhaps put a map of their building onto a web page – hardly cutting-edge technology.

There are a number of other resources that do extend the use of mapping services, some of which can have a use within a library or information environment. Frappr at **www.frappr.com** lets users create a map, and then add in pushpins to highlight particular areas. It's a useful way for a group to keep in contact, but it could also be used as a valuable information resource in its own right. For example, historical maps highlighting battlefields, places mentioned in Shakespeare or locations in Jane Austen's work could all be created without too much difficulty. Wayfaring at **www.wayfaring.com** works in a similar manner, with users creating maps and adding content that is personal to them. Other resources such as Trippermap at **www.trippermap.com** allow users to match their Flickr photographs to locations, while Placeopedia at **www.placeopedia.com** matches locations mentioned in the Wikipedia to a physical location.

Annotating web pages

We tend to think of web pages as fairly static, in the sense that we visit them, take information from them and leave. Even in a situation where there may be a chat box on a page that you can use to interact with other people, it's a chat box on a page that we still can't do anything with. However, more resources are coming on-stream that allow users to 'mark up' a web page in one way or another to share that information or opinion with other people. This can be done via services such as del.icio.us or Furl where we're able to comment, but that's still via another site, and not quite as helpful.

Wikalong

The Wikalong at **www.wikalong.org** works with the Firefox browser by embedding a sidebar in the browser window. When you visit a web page you want to comment on, you can simply add whatever you wish to say. When you visit that page again in the future you'll be able to see your comments, and share them with other people. There are a lot of ways in which a service like this can be used. Obviously you can simply add a little discussion or annotation to a page and leave it at that, but it could also be used in a 'see also' capacity. If you're training a group of people the Wikalong lets you, as the trainer, guide students around a number of web pages, making suggestions for what else they could look at, which links to click on, or what to make a note of to think about. It's unlikely that this resource would have widespread value, since a lot of people would need to use it and visit the same pages, but within a small community (such as a training group) all the users could be encouraged to get involved.

MyStickies

MyStickies at **www.mystickies.com** is designed to allow you to put little 'post it' notes on web pages which remain there until you delete them. The system also allows you to view all of your notes, categorize them and review, edit or delete them. At the moment the system works only with individual accounts, although the site does promise that the possibility for sharing stickies across different accounts and making them public is being actively developed. The resource could still be useful, however, if an account was created for a computer that was used at the reference desk, for example, and individual members of staff could add notes on the web pages or sites they come across.

Wizlite

Wizlite at **http://wizlite.com** is a collaborative web-page highlighting system. I'm sure you have used those colourful highlighter pens that allow you to mark up sections of a printed page for emphasis. If you can imagine being able to do this on a web page that's what Wizlite does, with the addition that you can then annotate what has been marked up on the page for other people to read. In order for the system to work it's necessary to create an account and download and install a Firefox extension - at the moment the system doesn't work with Microsoft Internet Explorer - and when you have done that you can start highlighting text on pages. This can then be shared with everyone or just a selected group of people.

Tagground

Tagground at **www.tagground.com** works in a slightly different way in that users input either a website address or a word to search on. The system then checks with various bookmarking services, such as del.icio.us, and pulls up a listing of tags that have been used to describe that particular page, or alternatively pages that use a specific tag. This can be a useful way of seeing how a group of (admittedly anonymous) users views a particular site, and finding websites using a serendipitous approach.

Clipmarks

Clipmarks at **http://clipmarks.com** is, as the name suggests, a clippings service. Users clip content (up to 2000 characters) on web pages that interests them and tag it as they feel appropriate, and it then gets posted directly to the Clipmarks site. There are various different categories to which clipped content can be assigned, and users can browse just those categories that interest them. The main disadvantage of a system like this is that there is very little control over what is posted, other than the 'wisdom of the crowd,' so it is best used for general browsing and keeping up to date with the latest fads and fancies that take people's interest.

Conversate

Conversate at **www.conversate.org** is a resource that lets users e-mail colleagues when they find a page that is of interest to them. Conversate then provides space for two or more people to discuss a page. Other than the initial e-mail to alert someone to a new conversation, discussion takes place on the Conversate site, ensuring that everything is kept in one place and not lost in a flood of e-mails.

Conclusion

Each of the sections covered here could all too easily be expanded into its own chapter. There are resources being created to answer questions that most of us haven't even thought of asking yet. Many of the resources in this chapter will not be widely used, but in all honesty I don't think that really matters to any great extent. If you and your user group find any of them helpful for whatever reason, then I'd certainly encourage you to make use of them.

URLs mentioned in this chapter

http://10minutemail.com/10MinuteMail/index.html
www.30gigs.com
http://allyourwords.com
www.amazon.co.uk
www.bebo.com
www.bitty.com
www.blogtronix.com
www.blyberg.net/card-generator
www.box.net
www.centraldesktop.com
www.chacha.com

http://cl1p.net

http://clipmarks.com

www.collectivex.com

www.connectviabooks.com

www.conversate.org

www.customsigngenerator.com

www.dabbledb.com

http://dailymashup.com

www.debbiesidea.com

www.dine52.com

http://docs.google.com

http://dodgeit.com

http://doggdot.us

www.frappr.com

http://futureme.org

www.goffice.com

http://indy.tv

www.jjchandler.com/tombstone

www.joyent.com

http://judgejohnroberts.com

www.last.fm

http://lib.rario.us

www.libraryforlife.org/blogs/lifeline/?p=2504

www.librarything.com

www.librarything.com/groups/librarianswholibrar

www.linkedin.com

http://literature-map.com

www.littlefunny.com/Google.aspx

www.littlefunny.com/ShowGoogle.aspx?logo=Librarians%20are%20gr
    eat!

www.liveplasma.com

http://logo54.com/net/yahoo

www.mailchimp.com

www.mailinator.com/mailinator/index.jsp

http://mailnull.com

www.meetup.com

www.mightyv.com

http://movielens.umn.edu/login

http://movies.ajaxilicious.be

http://multiply.com

www.music-map.com

http://myfilmz.net

www.myspace.com

www.mystickies.com

www.mywebdesktop.net

www.near-time.net

www.pandora.com

www.placeopedia.com

www.pookmail.com/about.php

www.slideshare.net

http://sneakemail.com

http://spambob.com

www.spamgourmet.com

www.spamhole.com/create.html

www.tagground.com/T/Default.aspx

www.tagworld.com

www.tempinbox.com/english

www.thinkfree.com

www.towncrossing.com

www.trippermap.com

www.tv.com

www.wayfaring.com

www.whatshouldireadnext.com

www.wikalong.org

http://wizlite.com

http://ww1.titantv.com

www.yousendit.com

www.zoho.com/virtual-office

Chapter 12

Implementing Web 2.0

Introduction

Much of this book has focused on the resources that are already available to the enthusiastic information professional, and I hope that you have been enthused and interested enough to try some of them for yourself already. One of the encouraging things about many of these products is that you can just do exactly that – register (and sometimes not even that), play around with them free of any cost implications, and just discard the ones that don't work for you, while continuing to use and benefit from those that are valuable.

Of course, it's very easy to do this on a personal level; all it takes is to put aside a small amount of time to try out a resource. While this may initially appear to be something of a case of 'easier said than done', I suspect that you'll quickly find that if you're sensible about your choice of product you will save yourself a lot of time. Once I started to use RSS feeds to keep up to date, I didn't need to waste precious time going from site to site to stay abreast of what was going on. Integrating feeds into a start page system so that I could immediately see the new headlines of key weblogs or searches also saved time, and links through to key resources meant that I wasn't constantly pulling down my Favorites menu. The time you have really does start to add up over the course of a week, and it's time that you can plough back to give yourself an extra five or ten minutes to try something new.

However, doing things on a personal level is very different to doing them in a corporate or organizational environment, where you may well have many conflicting demands on your time, with different user groups wanting different things and various individual users all at different levels of expertise, with different information requirements. In this final chapter I'll look at some of the things that must be considered when implementing new resources, and some tactics that you might want to consider employing, irrespective of the type of library you're in.

Library 2.0

When talking about Web 2.0 and utilizing it within a library context it's really not possible to do this without at least some mention of the term 'Library 2.0'. The term itself was defined by Michael Casey in his LibraryCrunch weblog at **www.librarycrunch.com**. His description considered the way in which libraries address the issue of Web 2.0 resources that have a role to play in an information setting, with libraries having to create and adopt a strategy to cope with change and incorporate new tools, and to encourage increased participation from library users.

Library 2.0 is still under much discussion, with some individuals arguing that this whole concept is not new at all, and that while some individual resources and utilities can enhance some services, these do not amount to a fundamental shift or change in the way in which users and communities can best be served: others argue that the number of resources available, and the way in which they are converging, is resulting in a new attitude towards the provision of information and the role of the end-user, leading to a new generation of library services. An overview of this discussion, with links to many articles that discuss it in depth, is to be found in the Wikipedia entry for Library 2.0, at **http://en.wikipedia. org/wiki/Library_2.0**. As usual in discussions of this nature both viewpoints hold considerable merit, and I suspect that the true answer lies somewhere in between, but it will take several years before we are able to view this debate accurately in retrospect.

My personal view is that a library or information centre is in the business of ensuring that its users are served as quickly and effectively as possible, using the most appropriate tools. As is self-evident from the rest of this book, there are lots of resources now available that can assist in this process, and I am less concerned with the specific terminology than in what these resources actually *are*, and how (and if) they can be used. It is my hope and expectation that a good information professional will be interested and intrigued enough to explore them, and then exploit those that provide additional benefit to them, either as an individual or as an information professional. In the final analysis, however, I am going to sit on the fence and leave it up to readers to decide for themselves.

Despite that statement, there are certain things that I feel that information professionals will need to consider when employing any of the resources mentioned in the book, either on an individual case-by-case basis, or as part of a blended approach.

Beta is forever

Beta testing really isn't a new concept – things are changing all the time. New versions of software are produced to fix bugs, to improve performance or to include new ideas or options; books come in different editions as the authors modify the content in the light of changing circumstances and information; and even cleaning products come branded as 'new and improved'. Things are constantly changing and evolving, but the two differences with the kind of resources that we're looking at here is both the rate and speed of change, and also the lack of control end-users have on the resources themselves.

As I mentioned in the preface of this book, it's been quite hard to write because new resources are constantly popping up or disappearing, and it's difficult to keep track of them all. I can take a screenshot of a product one day, only to visit the next to find that it has changed completely. Resources such as weblogs that combine content from different utilities are adding new ones, meaning that web authors can change the look and feel (and indeed purpose) of their weblogs with dizzying speed. In the 'old days' (however and whenever you define those) the rate of change was slower – a product could be used for several years before the next incarnation would be released, and so the rate of change was not as noticeable.

The fact that most Web 2.0 resources are free at the point of use also requires us to view them differently. In most instances we don't download software onto our own systems to use – the browser simply loads the software as necessary in conjunction with our operating system(s), and we use the product without giving that process a moment's thought. However, this does make us quite vulnerable since we can't keep a copy of the software as we can if we purchase something. As a result, the people who create the software can change the functionality at will, and users have little say in the matter. Consequently, not only do things change quickly, but we have no control over that change, which can be quite scary.

When I have demonstrated some of the products mentioned in this book to information professionals they have been enthusiastic, but often ask the question, 'This is all very well, but if I put a lot of time into a resource and it disappears, what am I left with?' This is a pertinent point. In most instances if a package is going to be retired the creators will give users time to save their data, or to export it to another product. When looking at which resource to use my feeling is that it's worth waiting a few months before deploying a product and relying on it. If you're able to make back-ups of your data, do just that, and on a regular basis.

If possible, either run two products in tandem or be aware of a competing product that you can move to if necessary. For example, if my main start page resource doesn't work for some reason, I have a second one that I can use – it didn't take more than a few minutes to create, it works in exactly the same way and, although I don't keep it as up to date, the functionality is good enough that I'm not particularly inconvenienced if there is unexpected downtime on my preferred package. It's also worth while watching to see if there are any enhancements to the product and, if so, how regular they are. A product that comes out and doesn't improve is either a product that answers a very specific need and simply does the job, or it's a product that the creators released in the hope that it would make a million dollars for them overnight, which is never the case.

It does pay to shop around between different products, read reviews of them and keep up to date on the competition. I agree this takes time, but in truth it is part of the professional updating process: a librarian in the role of facilitator should aim to make their users' lives easier, and this includes being able to recommend different answers to information requirements.

Don't expect perfection

It is always tempting, whatever we're doing, to keep working on something until we think that it's perfect and finished. There is nothing as satisfying as a job well done. However, within the Web 2.0 environment this is very far from the case. This is due in part to the climate in which products are released – there is a great deal of competition, and in most instances it does appear better (at least the creators of the products seem to think so) to release the software, get people using it, and then fix and improve things down the line. If I'm not paying for the use of a particular product I can't really complain about this – it is my choice to use something, but as part of the user community I know that I can help a product move forward by alerting the designers to errors or bugs, and to give them feedback on the product.

As librarians offering a service it is tempting to always try to ensure that it is in a 'finished' form that can be deployed and used without a hitch from day one. Clearly, if we're using resources that don't subscribe to the same tenets then there will inevitably be a discrepancy between the service we would like to provide, and the service that we are able to provide.

The extent to which this is acceptable will differ from professional to professional, organization to organization, and user to user; there is no right or wrong answer for every case. When rolling out a new product, however, I suggest a four-stage approach.

1   Spend some time looking at a specific product, watching to see if there are any enhancements, improvements, downtimes and criticisms of it.
2   Use the product either by yourself or in conjunction with colleagues, and if appropriate alongside any existing solutions. Monitor the use

of the new product, see if it does the job that you want, and check to see that it does actually save time or improve search results or whatever it is supposed to do.

3 Make users aware of the product, with or without fanfare, depending on your preference, and monitor use, checking with colleagues or users to gain their impressions of it. Make it clear that it is *a* solution to a problem, not *the* solution, and that its continued existence or development should not be taken as a given. In other words, don't hype the product and get users overly excited, since they are likely to remember failures more vividly than continued quiet successes.

4 Over time, once you and the user community gain confidence in the product, consider scaling back on any tandem solutions, particularly if the resource you are using does get purchased by one of the big corporations, such as Google or Yahoo!. Once that happens the product will almost certainly (with the emphasis on 'almost') have a long-term future as it becomes incorporated into the fold.

Staff involvement
Colleagues

While it would be a lovely situation if all members of staff were keen and enthusiastic, looking forward to coming into work each day with a bounce in their step and a smile on their lips ready to explore an exciting world of new products and challenges, it's simply not going to happen. It is unrealistic to expect colleagues to start using new products as soon as you have found them, however much time is saved, or however good they are at making people's lives easier; after all, everyone has their own job to do and most people don't have the time to innovate constantly. It may not be seen as exciting and challenging, and it may well be thought tiresome to use untried and untested products, with the probability of looking like a fool if things don't work out.

Consequently you need to ask yourself if your colleagues are ready to make a shift towards providing new resources in new ways. Disappointingly the answer is sometimes a resounding 'no', and the job at that point becomes one of encouraging a change in thinking and attitude, together with offering the carrot of enlightened self-interest. Here I include a personal anecdote. My brother is a recruitment consultant who needs to keep on top of everything that's happening in his field of interest. One afternoon I introduced him to the idea of a start page, together with some RSS feeds based on Google News searches. A couple of weeks later he started a new job, and his boss saw his start page and wanted to know more. Rick explained how it worked, and his boss asked, 'So can I keep a close eye on all our competitors that easily?'; within a week everyone in the company was using their own start page. Now, this happened in a company that doesn't have an information department and the people concerned were interested in recruitment, not information. However, once they could see the value of the resource on a personal level the take-up was almost instantaneous.

If possible, try to move from an existing resource to a Web 2.0 product yourself and simply point out to colleagues how much easier life has become. Encourage the use of collaborative tools, and share your work, such as word documents or presentations, via Google Docs or SlideShare and so on. There really isn't a need to make a great song and dance about it – just do it. If you're working with an end-user who is looking for some specific information, quickly create a custom-built search engine for them, then let them get on with it – they won't need a great deal of training or much by the way of introduction. If they like it, you can be sure they'll want other search engines, and they'll tell their colleagues. In other words, let your users set the pace, with encouragement from you.

Technical support colleagues

Another group of colleagues that may require specific handling is the technical support team. A keen and enthused technical support colleague can make the process of implementing technology a pleasurable and fun experience, but this can be a rare occurrence, and lack of interest on the part of technical support can be dispiriting.

Of course many Web 2.0 products don't actually require any involvement from technical staff at all – they are designed specifically for end-users to just get on and create something, without worrying about the intricacies of HTML, Flash, JavaScript or anything else. On the one hand, this is good news, because it means that technical support staff are not in a position to be an obstacle in the creation of the products, but, on the other hand, it's a foolish person who alienates their support department; they will still be needed! Much depends on the extent to which you are considering blending in new resources with existing ones – if you want to have an RSS feed of a weblog on your library home page, for example, technical support staff may well have to implement this.

Once again, there is no right or wrong answer on how you answer this problem, but it is one that you do need to be aware of. Perhaps talk to technical support staff casually to let them know that you're experimenting with new products and see if they're interested. If so, they may well suggest to you that it would be possible to use some of them in your existing setup. Alternatively point to other libraries that have embraced the concept and ask the technical support people (in all innocence, of course) how and if it would be possible for them to do the same thing.

Management

Management is of course probably the most difficult or tricky group to work with. You may find that you are expected to jump through hoops to try different things, or will be told that you cannot do something because it cannot be controlled or given a corporate look, feel or badge. It may be worth trying out something such as a podcast that is so radically different that it's not possible to fit it to an existing corporate style. Many other resources do allow users to change the look and feel, however, so it may be worth encouraging the technical support staff to get involved by altering a weblog or wiki template so that they look like any other page on the corporate website, for example.

Other resources may need to be viewed in the 'just do it' state of mind. Simply point out the benefits of using a product such as Flickr in the hope that these outweigh the lack of control or corporate style. Other products are available that staff may just be able to use without any interference from higher up in the organization, such as their own start pages, for example.

However, I would not want to entirely dismiss the point that if you intend to use Web 2.0 resources, and to involve and encourage both users and staff in a different way, this will have an effect on the organization as a whole. Equally, though, it's worth pointing out that the same discussions have been thrashed out with regards to using e-mail and the internet; the idea that a company should not use e-mail sounds as ridiculous now as not utilizing the resources mentioned in this book will do in two or three years' time.

Promoting a new approach

Once something new is suggested, be it the use of e-mail, creating a website or using the internet to obtain information, several things will happen straightaway. A small number of enthusiasts will quickly adopt the new resource, play with it and explore its potential. Other people will be quick to say that there is no value in the new resource, it's a waste of time, and people are better off using tried and traditional approaches. This is certainly true in the case of Web 2.0, as has previously been mentioned. You must be aware that not everyone is going to be keen, and the inadequacies and limitations of the resource may be pointed out.

You need to be in a position where you can address all of your users' concerns: be honest and up front, admit that the new resources are not a solution to the world's problems, and put people right if they make incorrect statements or unfounded criticisms. Be aware of and recognize the existence of what Brian Kelly refers to in his Web 2.0 Introduction presentation as 'librarian fundamentalists' (**www.ukoln.ac.uk/web-focus/events/seminars/cilip-ucrg-2006-12/ppt2000-html/intro_files/v3_document.html**). These individuals think they know best, believe that users need to learn Boolean search techniques, do not in fact want users to search for themselves and want services to be perfect before they are released.

The following is a list of some ideas to consider when utilizing and promoting Web 2.0 based resources. Some may not be appropriate for your own situation, so do feel free to pick, mix, match or discard!

1   Consider what resources you currently use, and see if any of those can be better served by switching to a Web 2.0 resource.

2   Look at existing users and see what information needs they have; can any of these be serviced via some of the utilities mentioned in this book?

3   What outreach services does the information centre currently offer? Can access to IM or chat resources provide more access to information professionals?

4   What clubs, user groups, activities or events does the library currently get involved with? Could any of these benefit from the addition of more information made available by the utilization of customized search engines, for example?

5   Can you use simple resources such as Flickr to add a new dimension to existing resources, even with something as straightforward as creating a photographic record of an event?

6   Try to turn existing, enthusiastic users of your services into publishing colleagues by getting them involved in community-based resources, such as portal services, commenting on weblog entries, linking their own resources to yours.

7   Do the same thing differently – produce information posters using some of the image-generator products, for example.

8   Encourage feedback in any format, but particularly via the resource itself, such as comments on a weblog, amended entries in a wiki and so on.

9   Use a resource for a specific period of time, such as creating a customized search engine to provide data for a particular event, be it sporting, political or cultural, and brand it as such. Of course, if it proves popular it doesn't actually need to be withdrawn at the conclusion of the event.

10 Encourage 'play'. The use of this word tends to trivialize an important concept, but it's widely understood, so get staff and users to simply try things out to see if they work. Finding that something doesn't work is as important as finding things that do, so try to encourage that idea.

11 Get users to suggest things. It's simply not possible for one person, or even a group of people, to keep on top of everything being produced, and so get your users to suggest things – create a virtual 'suggestion box' via a wiki or portal weblog, for example.

12 Be open-minded. There are a lot of resources that at first glance may seem to have no value whatsoever. A good example here is Second Life at **http://secondlife.com**, which is an online interactive community in which people create avatars and 'live' in a virtual society. There are currently over 2 million 'residents' in Second Life, and this includes a flourishing library which runs various events of a cultural and educational nature. There are many ways in which this system could be used within a library – as an easy-to-control virtual meeting-room environment, for example.

13 Mix and match resources. One of the useful things about a lot of Web 2.0 resources is that they can be used in various different combinations. A widget may be used on a web page, or as a module in a start page, or on a weblog or in a portal, for example. This flexibility enables the use of products in new and different ways – quite often ways never considered by the original designers. If you can't use a resource one way, see if it can be used in another.

Keeping current

I'm sure that by now you should have no problems working out how to remain current with developments in this subject area by using your own search engines, start pages, RSS feeds and so on. However, a few resources are worth pointing out. There are a great many directories that just list Web 2.0 resources, or perhaps provide brief commentary about them, such as the Web 2.0 directory at **www. econsultant.com/web2** or my own 'I want to' collection at **www.philb.com/iwantto.htm**. Emily Chang's eHub is a well researched collection of new resources at **www.emilychang.com/go/ehub**.

There are a great many weblogs that focus almost entirely on Web 2.0 matters, and quite simply the best way of finding them is to run a search using your preferred search engine. Many librarians are now writing about Web 2.0 and/or Library 2.0 as well, and their resources are a fount of useful data. It's worth looking at Liszen at **www.liszen.com** and LibWorm at **www.libworm.com**, since they are both resources that index hundreds of librarian-oriented weblogs. If you use Pageflakes (or even if you don't) you may find the small collection of librarian weblogs that I have put together to be of some use (**www.pageflakes.com/philipbradley.ashx?page=4541261**), and if you're based in the UK, or have an interest in British librarianship, you might want to visit or indeed join the British Librarian Bloggers Google group at **http://groups.google.com/group/britlibblogs**.

Another useful resource is going to be whatever it happens to be that you're using! By this I mean that if you make a lot of use of a resource such as Squidoo, it's worth doing a search to see what lenses exist in the Web 2.0 area (and there are a lot of them), or, if you use Zimbio as a portal service, explore that to see if there is anything that you find useful.

Don't forget to create some RSS feeds from your favourite search engines on specific aspects of Web 2.0 and bring them into your start page or incorporate them into your news aggregator, weblog or home (web) page.

Finally, don't forget to spend some time now and then visiting the website for this book, and if you come across any other resources that you think others would find useful, do consider getting involved and posting them. You can find more about the website in the Appendix.

Conclusion

So, in conclusion both to this chapter and to the book as a whole, where have we got to? Does such a thing as Web 2.0, Library 2.0 or indeed Librarian 2.0 actually exist, or is it all smoke and mirrors as some suggest? I believe that it's up to each one of us to make up our own minds, but I hope that you have found some resources to use on an ongoing basis that will allow you to do something new, or differently.

In my experience, librarians are perfect guests at a party – they're interesting, informed, open, curious and always want to know new things. There is no doubt that, whatever you call these new resources, they are a new way of doing things. This of course means that we need to stop doing old things, or at the very least adapt them into new formats. Excitingly, however, we do now have more tools that we can use to reach out to users, to inform them, assist them and to make things better.

If each of us can make one thing a little better, then consider what changes we can all make between us – what job could offer more?

URLs mentioned in this chapter

www.econsultant.com/web2

www.emilychang.com/go/ehub

http://en.wikipedia.org/wiki/Library_2.0

http://groups.google.com/group/britlibblogs

www.librarycrunch.com

www.libworm.com

www.liszen.com

www.pageflakes.com/philipbradley.ashx?page=4541261

www.philb.com/iwantto.htm

http://secondlife.com

www.ukoln.ac.uk/web-focus/events/seminars/cilip-ucrg-2006-
    12/ppt2000-html/intro_files/v3_document.html

Appendix
The companion website

Introduction

As I have already mentioned, it's virtually impossible to keep up to date with everything that is happening within the Web 2.0 arena. Moreover, as we're all aware, a print product will be out of date very quickly - in all probability before the title gets to the printers. A common and not unfair criticism of most books that relate to some aspect of the internet is 'it's already out of date'. This is annoying for the readers, who excitedly copy a link to their browser only to find that a URL is dead or changed, and it's even more infuriating for the authors of such books. I often feel that I should produce little stickers with updated URLs that can be stuck into the books that I've written!

However, with the advent of Web 2.0 we are at last in a position where the problem of currency is less of an issue than it has been in the past. It is now perfectly possible to create a website and let the readers of the book get involved in a rather more interesting and exciting way than just reading it. Not only does it mean that I as the author can update and amend any errant URLs that have the temerity to change, but you as the reader can do exactly the same thing. Moreover, if either of us finds new resources, or updates, or has comments to make regarding the content of a chapter, it's now possible to share that information. Of course, I'm talking here as though there are just the two of us, but in truth (at least, I hope so) there will be several thousand of us, who have come together in a community based around this particular book. Between us we should create a resource that is current and informative, and supplements the information contained in the book.

How to use Web 2.0 in your library – the portal

I spent some time considering which resource to use in order to create the website. I wanted a resource that people could view easily, that readers could, if they wished, get involved with, and that provides a variety of different functions. Eventually I decided to create a Zimbio portal, and you can find it at **www.zimbio.com/portal/How+to+use+Web+2.0+in+your+library** – this is a fairly horrible URL, so feel free to use **http://doiop.com/web20** or **http://tinyurl.com/ybmx4e** instead, whichever you prefer. A screen-shot of the page is shown in Figure A.1.

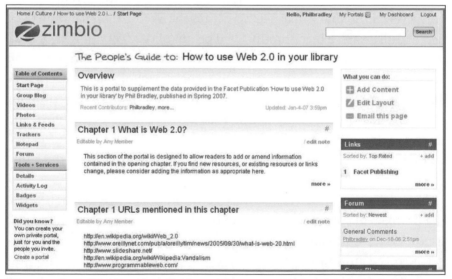

Figure A.1 The People's Guide to *How to use Web 2.0 in your library*

Chapter notes

The portal is composed of several different elements. Each chapter has two sections, the first being a general note area that can be edited by anyone who has registered with Zimbio, and can be used if you wish to make readers aware of any changes to the content of that chapter, such as the fact that a resource has changed its functionality, or if you have found another or a new resource that does the same job as one mentioned. Consequently, it supplements the information in the chapter. The second chapter note is a listing of URLs from the book. This allows users to get quicker access to the sites mentioned without having to go through the tedious process of typing out each URL from scratch. If a URL has changed or been updated, please feel free to add this information, but don't delete the original entry since people will not necessarily be able to follow the changes. An amendment should therefore look something like this:

> www.examplewebsite.com/url.htm This has now changed to www.examplewebsite.com/newurl.htm

Links module

There is a separate module for links. Use this for links that you find of a more general nature, such as a Web 2.0 directory, or a particularly useful weblog, or an example of a library that's doing something interesting.

Forum module

The forum is designed to be available to all the readers of this book and visitors to the site. If you want to make a comment, ask a question, start a debate or provide your own opinion, please do! I'm sure I don't need to remind you to observe netiquette and not to engage in anti-social behaviour or use abusive or 'not safe for work' language. This is as much as anything else an experiment in 'radical trust', as mentioned in Chapter 1, and I hope will be successful.

Weblog module

The portal also has a group blog, and you are encouraged to use this to add any new information that you'd like to make people aware of. You may, for example, be a librarian and have created an interesting resource that you'd like to publicize – this would be a great place to put that sort of information.

Other modules

Other modules are available, and if you want to add video material or photographs, or create new notes, please feel free to do so. Once again, all I ask is that you are respectful of the community as a whole.

Promoting the portal

If you would like to link to the portal, or make use of the RSS feed, you are welcome to do so, and indeed positively encouraged!

Conclusion

I hope that you will find *How to Use Web 2.0 in Your Library* useful, and the website just as helpful. Please do consider using it, as your input will improve both the website and future editions of this book. So stop by every now and then and add something new!

Index